STAGES ON LIFE'S WAY

▟ Foundations series

Testifying to the faith and creativity of the Orthodox Christian
Church, the Foundations series draws upon the riches of its
tradition to address the modern world. These survey texts are
suitable both for preliminary inquiry and deeper investigation,
in the classroom or for personal study.

Peter C. Bouteneff
Series Editor

Stages on Life's Way

ORTHODOX THINKING
ON BIOETHICS

Book 1 of the Foundations series

John & Lyn Breck

ST VLADIMIR'S SEMINARY PRESS
CRESTWOOD, NEW YORK
2005

Library of Congress Cataloging-in-Publication Data

Breck, John, 1939–
  Stages on life's way : Orthodox thinking on bioethics / John Breck & Lyn Breck.
    p. cm. — (Foundations ; bk. 1)
  ISBN–13: 978–0–88141–299–4 (alk. paper)
  ISBN–10: 0–88141–299–6 (alk. paper)
    1. Bioethics—Religious aspects—Orthodox Eastern Church. 2. Orthodox
Eastern Church—Doctrines. 3. Medical ethics—Religious apects—Orthodox
Eastern Church. 4. Spiritual life—Orthodox Eastern Church. I. Breck, Lyn.
II. St. Vladimir's Orthodox Theological Seminary (Crestwood, Tuckahoe,
Westchester County, N.Y.) III. Title. IV. Series: Foundations (St. Vladimir's
Orthodox Theological Seminary (Crestwood, Tuckahoe, Westchester County,
N.Y.)) ; bk. 1.
  [DNLM: 1. Bioethical Issues. 2. Eastern Orthodoxy.   WB 60 B829s 2005]
R725.56.B73 2005
174'.957—dc22

                                                              2005027259

© 2005 BY JOHN AND LYN BRECK

ST VLADIMIR'S SEMINARY PRESS
575 Scarsdale Rd, Crestwood, NY 10707
1-800-204-2665
www.svspress.com

ISSN 1556–9837
ISBN 0–88141–299–6
ISBN 978–0–88141–299–4

PRINTED IN THE UNITED STATES OF AMERICA

For
Margaret Pitts Kleiber
and
Helen Forgham Neville,
with gratitude and love

CONTENTS

foreword

Our being made in God's image is both a gift and a calling. Every human being bears the divine image as an inalienable gift, but we must work to attain to that image until it is truly a divine likeness. Living into the image of God involves living in accordance with our Christian faith. For faith is more than a consolation in the face of a death-bound world, and it is more than a series of teachings; it is a conviction about absolute reality, and it must penetrate the very fabric of our lives.

Harmonizing faith and life is a perpetual task entailing self-examination and the reorientation of our life, thoughts, and actions in the context of the sacramental life of the Church. But we also need some very specific help in making the connections between the Church's theology—gleaned from Holy Scripture as read in the light of Church tradition—and the often complex situations that life puts before us.

The field of ethics, from a Christian perspective, is concerned precisely with making those connections. Ethics is about applying the revealed truth about God, the world, and the human person to situations within the context of our daily lives, in all of their complexity and ambiguity. For these connections are not always apparent or easy to draw. It's one thing to apply "thou shalt not steal" to the workplace. But how do we apply Christian anthropology to the situation of a relative suffering from Alzheimer's and now requiring a respirator to sustain her life? How do we enter into the charged debate about stem cell research? How, in a world which concocts more and more elaborate means of dehumanization, do we live a life that reflects the image of God in us, a life that reflects genuine personhood?

In articles and books dating from the late 1980s onward, Fr John Breck, a pastor and New Testament scholar, has been wrestling with ethical questions, taking his place among the handful of Orthodox ethicists who emerged in the late twentieth century.[1] In his written output as well as in classrooms in the United States and in Europe, Fr John has been working to engage the absolute teachings of the Church with human situations. In so doing, he consistently reminds us that in Orthodox teaching, the human person is a continuity from conception to resurrection. That means that before, during, and after a person's earthly life in a body that breathes oxygen, we are dealing with a being created in God's image and whose life has ultimate value.

In this volume, Fr John sets out a series of reflections that takes us along the stages in that continuum. In these pages, we find a wealth of information and practical advice for readers seeking to apply their faith to their lives. But we also have here a series of case studies on how an Orthodox Christian can find his or her way in the world, how Orthodox Christians "do" bioethics.

---

[1]Other Orthodox authors published in this field include Stanley Harakas, Alexander Webster, Christos Yannaras, Tristram Engelhardt, Vigen Guroian, and Joseph Woodill.

Here are some of the principles that emerge, both implicitly and explicitly, in the pages of this book:

* ✱ "Orthodox ethics" is primarily a goal-oriented vocation, rather than an application of rules. Even the titles of Orthodox ethical reflections are indicative of this: *Towards Transfigured Life* (Harakas), *The Freedom of Morality* (Yannaras), *God with Us* (Breck). Orthodox ethics shows us what redeemed humanity looks like and orients us in that direction. Orthodox ethics is not so much proscriptive ("thou shalt not") as indicative ("thou ought" or "behold the goal!").

* ✱ Orthodox ethics draws on the teachings of the Church. This is not as obvious as it may sound, for many of the ethical decisions before us today—involving, for example, cloning, stem cells, or eugenics—were not envisioned during the formative periods of the Church's teaching on the human person. This means that we have to acquire a "scriptural mind" and a "patristic mind"; we have to become so steeped in the tradition of the Church that our thinking naturally takes its contours. In this way, even situations that were unforeseeable to the ancients can be informed by the foundations they laid.

* ✱ In order properly to do ethics, and especially bioethics as helpfully defined in the early pages of Fr John's introduction, we need to be conversant with science. To negotiate our way through, for example, questions about abortion, birth control, and reproductive

technologies, we need to consider when human life can properly be said to begin. This in turn requires a thoughtful engagement with the empirical sciences, an engagement that runs consistently through the history of the Church's theological reflection, ancient and modern.

Having said this, ethical dilemmas posed to us today are complex and delicate. There are no canons about cloning, *in vitro* fertilization, or, for that matter, the possibility of extraterrestrial life. This means that ethics consists in the art of applying timeless principles to time-bound situations. Orthodox ethics constantly strives to strike the right relationship between the absolute and the situational, between universal, unchanging, timeless truths and guidelines, and the particular, variable, and sometimes terribly messy situations before us at a given moment.

All of this means that any good Christian ethicist needs to be courageous, because this struggle for balance, a struggle which involves situations that are very close to our hearts—reproduction, sexual orientation and expression, illness, death and dying—is often going to result in an unpopular stance. A good ethicist is likely to get attacked from all sides: for not being absolute enough, for not being understanding or permissive enough. What he or she needs is not our attacks but our prayers and the sharing of our experience and understanding, for ethics is also an ecclesial undertaking.

As ecclesial or communal as ethics may be, we still need people with the courage, the theological sense, and the scientific acumen to make the necessary connections for us, and even to show us how we might make some of the connections ourselves, so that our own decisions, our own lives, may truly reflect our faith. May this book be such a contribution.

A word is in order about the contribution to this book by Lyn Breck (chap. 5). Lyn's background as an instructor in spirituality in a seminary context directly influenced her interest in applied, as distinguished from theoretical, spirituality, in behavior versus concepts. She is drawn toward questions such as, How do we live our lives? What are our ethical choices? and How do these choices foster our witness to God's kingdom and its reality among us? For many years a counselor and retreat leader within the Orthodox Church, she is especially poised to make an Orthodox contribution to thinking about addictions and family systems. Such reflection is indispensable, for if bioethics has to do with living a right life and with reflecting in ourselves and in our relationships the image of God, then due attention needs to be paid to those behaviors and patterns which distort the image in particular and damaging ways. We need to alert ourselves to the phenomenon of addiction—an awareness of which has increased in many circles but remains dormant in others—and to learn about helping ourselves and others in the way of recovery.

As in the rest of the book, we are again shown the importance of drawing, though not uncritically, on secular medical and behavioral sciences in order to benefit from their empirical, practical evidence. Some may complain that the Fathers didn't talk about addictions and dysfunctions and that therefore to concern ourselves with them is an enslavement to modern secular thinking. Well, the Fathers talked a great deal about the passions, and that is precisely the sphere within which we ought to consider addictions, compulsions, and dysfunctional patterns of behavior and relationships. Much of what Lyn Breck writes here is not exclusively Orthodox; it is practical information available to all from a wide variety of sources. (Many of these sources, especially those from Twelve Step programs, bear a strong spiritual component.) But given what we now know about brain chemistry, as well as about addictions, Orthodox thinking on bioethics can no longer go without addressing this dimension of human experience.

—Peter C. Bouteneff

acknowledgments

The authors are grateful for the thoughtful and gentle editing of Michael Breck, Al Rossi, Brian Phipps, and Peter Bouteneff.

introduction

BIOETHICS AND THE
STAGES ON LIFE'S WAY

Over the past three decades, bioethics has seized the popular imagination like almost nothing else, especially throughout the developed world. Newspapers and talk shows dwell on a multitude of bioethical issues, while both secular and religious journals attempt to keep up with and to evaluate the implications of those issues for our lives and our future. What is this phenomenon known as bioethics, and how does it affect us, our families, and the society in which we live?

Developed from the mid-1960s, bioethics is usually described as a discipline that evaluates the moral implications of recent developments in medical research and the applications of those developments, particularly as they concern the beginning and end of human life. It deals with matters such as new procreative technologies, the status of the human embryo, genetic engineering, contraception, and abortion. Then it moves on to consider matters such as the definition of death, organ donation, and care for the terminally ill, including the headline-grabbing topics of euthanasia and physician-assisted suicide.

Considered in this narrow perspective, the field of bioethics calls up within us a sense of ambivalence. On the one hand, it seems to be an esoteric discipline, with its own vocabulary and presup-positions, which is best left to the experts. On the other, we have the disquieting feeling that somehow it concerns us directly and personally, and that it represents both a promise and a threat. Its focus, after all, is not human life in the abstract but *my* life, *our* lives, as a member of social, ecclesial, and familial communities.

Who makes judgments concerning medical intervention at the beginning and end of life, and what criteria do they use? How will the decisions of specialists determine the way I and my family are treated in the maternity ward, in the emergency room, or in the geriatrics clinic? How can we defend ourselves and those we love from the invasiveness of medical decisions and technologies if their effect is to create or terminate lives in ways that run counter to our most deeply held beliefs?

Bioethicists are supposed to help us understand and evaluate newly developed medical technologies and procedures that can be applied at either end of life's spectrum. For Christians, this means they are to provide us with information and guidelines that will enable us to discern the will of God regarding the way our bio-logical existence should come into being and how it is most appropriately to end. It is an awesome task, one that involves not only the specialists but also each of us. This is because, in St Paul's language, we are "members of one another" (Rom 12.5). As such, we are responsible before God for each other's welfare, from conception to the grave and beyond.

Yet bioethics can also be seen as a broader framework that encom-passes not only the beginning and end of human life but also what Danish philosopher Søren Kierkegaard, in a very different vein, spoke of as "stages on life's way." For many years, I have taught courses in bioethics to seminarians—men and women preparing to enter the Orthodox priesthood or to assume other responsibilities within the Church. I have encouraged my students to expand the notion of bioethics well beyond the scope one expects to find in a standard bioethics textbook. Ethics is basically a descriptive discipline that evaluates human behavior. It considers the causes and effects of our actions, and it lays the foundation on which we construct moral judgments. It raises questions about what is good and bad, right and wrong, appropriate and inappropriate. And it helps us to understand our moral duties and obligations—how we should shape our attitudes and how we should act. Bioethics is an extension of this concern, one that concentrates particularly on the *bios*, the physical, emotional, and psychological aspects of human existence. This means that bioethical issues properly include not only the inception and close of our lives but also the various stages that mark our journeys throughout our lifetimes.

Acquiring the Mind of the Church

How indeed is the Church to respond to the awesome challenges posed by recent developments in the burgeoning field of biomedical technology? How do we as pastors and other members of the body of Christ provide adequate and faithful answers to questions that, until the middle of the last century, had never even been posed? Most of us, of course, have no formal medical training. Consequently, we have very limited means for assessing the moral implications of today's "new medicine." Embryologists are still arguing over the point at which human life actually begins and what this means for the manipulation of the human embryo.

Molecular biologists are discovering new ways to control genes, and some would offer us the ability to select the sex or other characteristics of our offspring to create "designer babies." Neurologists are devising ever more sophisticated techniques for blocking nerve paths to provide relief to patients in chronic pain. And gerontologists are scrutinizing chromosomal telomeres[1] and other phenomena that affect the aging process, in an effort to extend life spans by a third or more.

Such people are highly trained specialists, and most of us don't count ourselves among their number. Yet as priests and concerned laypersons, we are frequently called on to offer guidance—to medical professionals, to patients and their families, and to the public—regarding the moral consequences of such research. It's a daunting challenge, one that requires us to become conversant with medical technology and its potential for good and ill, while we ground our reflection ever more deeply in Holy Scripture and in Holy Tradition. Scripture and Tradition will not give us pat answers to questions concerning the use of specific, newly developed medical technologies. But they will provide us with the perspective—the "mind of the Church," shaped by Scripture and the whole of ecclesial tradition—needed to make moral judgments and to offer pastoral direction to those who are involved firsthand with critical issues.

To form that ecclesial mind, we need to return to the sources of our faith. For our purposes, this means returning to the foundational themes of Orthodox anthropology, to set forth once again

[1]Telomeres are the ends or tips of chromosomes, whose progressive shortening affects, and perhaps effects, the aging process.

the Church's teaching on the human person, created in the image of God and called to grow toward the divine likeness, the likeness of the Holy Trinity.

Divine and Human Personhood

The Christian understanding of God is based on personal and ecclesial experience. We obtain knowledge of God by means of revelation: in the Old Testament witness to his mighty acts throughout the history of Israel, in the New Testament witness to the person and work of Christ, and in the ongoing development of Holy Tradition within the life of the Christian community. Behind each of these witnesses, guaranteeing their authority and truth, is God himself in the person of the Holy Spirit. The Spirit preserves and discloses, in the Church and in personal experience, what Jesus refers to in the Gospel of John as "all the truth" (Jn 16.13–15). That fullness of truth provides us with a paradoxical image of God, one the mind can fathom and explain only to a limited extent and with the greatest difficulty.

On the one hand, God makes himself known as the creator and Lord of the natural order, both macrocosmos and microcosmos. God is thus the creative and sustaining power behind all things, from galaxies to elementary particles. Remarkable scientific tools, such as the Hubble space telescope and the electron microscope, reveal ever further the vastness and complexity of his handiwork. Scientists have good reason to believe that there exist incomprehensible phenomena such as "dark matter" and "dark energy" that constitute all but about 4 percent of material reality. They are also investigating the possible existence of parallel universes, extra dimensions beyond space and time. Others are probing into the nanosphere, the realm of the unimaginably small, while still others are exploring the mysteries of the human cell, a universe in itself. God indeed is Lord, and through the vastness and splendor of the created order, he makes himself known in all his power and majesty.

On the other hand, God reveals himself in weakness, poverty, and humility. He makes himself known and accessible in the person and witness of Jesus of Nazareth, whom the Church recognizes and proclaims to be divine, one of the Holy Trinity. Jesus reveals the one whom he calls Father to be the true father, the source and sustainer, of every human person. He makes God known as redeemer as well as creator, who by virtue of his self-sacrificing love offers to each person participation in God's own transcendent life. The God who creates and sustains all things is also the Father who loves all things and strives to draw every human person into an eternal communion with himself. The ascetic tradition of the Church will even claim, on grounds of personal experience, that God in his infinite love and compassion is closer to us than our own hearts.

This God of the macro and the micro, who knows us more intimately than we know ourselves, is by his very nature a God of personal communion. The Church's teaching on the Holy Trinity attempts to spell out the nature of this communion. God within his innermost being and reality is not a monolith but a triunity of divine persons—Father, Son, and Spirit—who dwell together in a relationship of mutual, inexhaustible love. That love, the patristic tradition insists, is so great that it overflows the limits of divine life to embrace and fill the entire creation, and first of all human persons, who are made "in the image and likeness of God" (Gen 1.26). God, therefore, is the archetype, as well as the source and fulfillment, of every personal human existence.

Contemporary Orthodox theologians describe personhood as "Being in communion." This describes the inner relationships of the Holy Trinity as well, God in his innermost being (*ad intra*). We are persons, truly personal beings, insofar as we reflect the personal qualities of Father, Son, and Spirit that unite them in an eternal communion of being and action. These include first of all the quality of *agapē*, or disinterested, self-sacrificing love. Therefore, personhood—what makes us "beings in communion" rather than mere individuals—is a quality bestowed on us by God. God, and not social convention or our genetic legacy, determines our personhood. It is God who confers on each human individual qualities and capacities that reflect his own, beginning with the quality of "person" and the capacity for self-giving love. We are who we are as persons to the degree that we reflect in our being and actions the personal, communal relationship of love that exists between the Father, the Son, and the Holy Spirit.

Yet this implies that human personhood is more than natural, a mere function of our physical being bounded by time and space. The very fact that God bestows on us the quality of "person" means that our lives are endowed with transcendent meaning and a destiny that lies beyond the limits of earthly existence. The end and fulfillment of human life—life's basic purpose—is to grow from earthly life, through physical death, into eternal life in the kingdom of God. It is to pass beyond the limits of biological existence and to participate in the eternal life of the Holy Trinity. To achieve this end, however, it is necessary to grow as well "from image to likeness," from our natural state, as created in the divine image, to a personal state of sanctification or holiness. St John of Damascus († ca. 749), the great synthesizer of Orthodox patristic theology, offers the classical definition of these terms: "*According to the image* refers to the intellect (reason) and freewill, whereas *according to the likeness* refers to our capacity to resemble God through the acquisition of virtue."[2] Movement from one to the other necessarily involves us in an ongoing ascetic struggle against the passions—against negative impulses such as lust, greed, anger, and jealousy, which invade and corrupt the human soul. The aim of this struggle is to acquire, by the indwelling power of the Holy Spirit, what the Fathers of the Church term *theōsis* or "deification": salvation by grace (alone!) that enables us to share in God's eternal life and being.

Only God can save us; we cannot save ourselves. This is the basic truth of the gospel. Nevertheless, we have to respond to God's saving initiative with an ongoing attitude of repentance, together with gestures of compassion, mercy, and love. These are "the good works which God prepared beforehand, that we should walk in them" (Eph 2.10). This response in the form of repentance and good works, by which we gradually acquire what are ultimately divine virtues, is what constitutes the moral life. We become moral, we grow toward the likeness of God, by behaving

---

[2]John of Damascus *On the Orthodox Faith* 2.12 (Migne, PG 94.920B). This distinction between image and likeness was not in the mind of the writer of Gen 1.26. There, the terms are most likely intended to be synonyms, according to the laws of Hebrew parallelism ("in our image" / "according to our likeness"). Numerous patristic witnesses make this distinction, however, and it carries over into contemporary Orthodox moral theology.

in a moral way. Yet paradoxically, we can behave morally only insofar as the capacity to do so is granted to us by God. The ability to behave in a moral way, a way truly pleasing to God, is one only God can confer on us. The Christian moral life, in other words, like faith itself, is a divine gift. We can know God as Father only through Jesus Christ, and we are able to pursue the likeness of God only through the sanctifying work of the Holy Spirit within us.

Every human creature, without exception, is created in the image of God. Patristic tradition understands this image to be indelible. While it can be tarnished and obscured by sin, it can never be obliterated, not even in the most corrupt soul. The image, therefore, refers to an aspect of human nature, what establishes us as inherently and immutably human. The likeness of God, on the other hand, refers to the vocation of the human person, called to assume the spiritual struggle, the "unseen warfare," that leads to acquisition of divine virtues (justice, truth, beauty, mercy, love) and ultimately to *theōsis*, or communion in divine life. Created in the image of God, we are called to assume the likeness of God. This interplay between image and likeness is what gives meaning and purpose to our existence. The fact, then, that God is both the origin and ultimate end of human life means that Orthodox anthropology will stress a fundamental truth that bears directly on the question of how that life should be treated, including the limits to which it may be acceptably manipulated. This is the simple but profoundly important truth that *every human person is of infinite value and is therefore worthy of infinite compassion.*

Culture of Death or Culture of Life?

Given this basic conviction, the question remains as to who actually qualifies as a human person. Is that hallowed designation restricted to adults who are capable of acting rationally and autonomously? Or does it include the mentally and physically disabled, dependent children, and even those who have not yet emerged from the womb? This leads to the question of when human life begins, and whether that life at its earliest stages can be properly qualified as personal.

Yet it also takes us beyond that question to consider every aspect of life, every stage in human growth and development. Ethical reflection in recent times has focused almost exclusively on the beginning and end of life, and for very specific reasons. Government and the media have understandably obsessed over embryonic stem cell research and euthanasia. Already England and the Netherlands have passed laws sanctioning each of these, and pressures to do the same in the United States are growing relentlessly. As Pope John Paul II so often insisted, ours is a "culture of death," a designation equally applicable to nations of every continent on earth. Consider ethnic cleansing in Bosnia, Kosovo, and the Darfur region of Sudan, or the beheading of criminals and captives of terrorists in the Middle East, or the "disappearances" of those who oppose governments or drug cartels in South America, or the complicity of England and other countries in the "preemptive" war in Iraq. Then consider the fact that the United States is not the only country that puts to death the criminals in its midst, or encourages a runaway gun culture, or legalizes the murder of children in the womb. All of this, in addition to the deadly abuse heaped on animals by the cosmetics industry, on human embryos by the pharmaceuticals industry, and on the infirm elderly by those they inconvenience. Ours is indeed a culture of death, and we fixate with reason on the smallest and most vulnerable of its members.

Nonetheless, it is also a culture of life, in which countless people offer gestures of self-sacrificing love to those they barely know—in hospitals, in schools, on the battlefield, in coastlands ravaged by tsunamis, or in the Twin Towers. I was in LaGuardia Airport when the lights went out in the 2003 breakdown of electric grids throughout the northeast and central parts of the country. The demonstrations of care and civility shown in that critical time matched those made by New Yorkers during the disaster of September 11th. Other such signs abound. Abused children are taken in by concerned relatives or are cared for by compassionate social workers. People who could be earning small fortunes in industry spend their time, with little financial reward, counseling those addicted to alcohol and other drugs, while nurturing their codependent family members. Nurses and other medical professionals tend to the needs of the sick and lonely, not so much for a paycheck as to render a real and precious service to those less fortunate than themselves. Charities flourish. Hospices abound. And Christian missionaries are rebuilding the spiritual infrastructure of places like Albania, are creating seminaries and medical clinics throughout Africa, and are otherwise living, as well as proclaiming, the gospel of peace.

Gestures such as these go a long way toward countering the culture of death. In each person who performs such gestures, they serve as an irrefutable witness to the reality of the image of God in the inner depths both of themselves and of those to whom they minister.

The Path Ahead

In the following chapters, we begin with an overview of some of the most important bioethical problems we face today in the United States and throughout the world. This will be followed by reflections on the mystery, or sacrament, of Christian marriage, together with the sensitive matters of sexuality and sexual expression. Then we turn to the critical and divisive issue of the use and abuse of human embryos, looking especially at their potential for providing therapies that can cure some of the most devastating illnesses we now face, including HIV infection and neurological diseases such as Parkinson's and Alzheimer's. From there, we move on to further stages in the growth and development of the human person. These include proper care offered to newborns, including the physically and mentally disabled. They also include the dysfunctional dynamic that governs family systems, together with the delicate and often burdensome task of recognizing, acknowledging, and treating addictive behaviors. Because my wife, Lyn Breck, has worked professionally for many years in the field of addictions and has specialized in family-systems therapy, I have invited her to write this particular chapter. Moving to the last stage along life's journey, we take up the mystery of death, particularly as it is presented in the thought of the apostle Paul. Finally, I will offer some thoughts regarding our responsibilities in caring for the terminally ill, including the comatose and those diagnosed as being in a persistent vegetative state.

In each instance, our concern is to examine the various questions we will raise less from a strictly ethical point of view and more in the light of what Orthodox theology has to say about God, the human person, and the world we live in. The chapter on the use and abuse of human embryos is unavoidably technical. For this reason, I have included with it a brief glossary of some key terms used in the field of embryology. The other chapters should prove more accessible to readers who have no special training in science or medicine.

Our concern, then, is to look at a spectrum of stages on life's way, beginning with the creation of human life, passing from infancy through adulthood, and closing with the silence of death. Each of these stages can mark a paschal moment in our lives, a moment that unites us intimately and personally with Christ's passion, death, and resurrection. Each stage challenges us as members of the Christian community to "offer ourselves, and each other, and our whole life to Christ our God."[3] This is our fundamental spiritual calling: to bring one another, from the womb to the tomb, into the light and life of the resurrected Lord. At the same time, it describes our basic moral obligation to acknowledge—through attitudes, words, and gestures—the beauty and majesty of the divine image in every human person, and to devote ourselves to that person with the same love that God has so richly poured into our own hearts by the presence and power of his Holy Spirit.

[3]A common petition in Orthodox litanies.

chapter one

BIOETHICAL CHALLENGES IN THE NEW MILLENNIUM

There's a battle outside, and it's raging.
—Bob Dylan, "The Times They Are A-Changin' "

The soul's war with the enemy lasts until death.
—Staretz Silouan, in *St Silouan the Athonite*

With the recent sequencing of the human genome, development of radically new reproductive techniques, including cloning, and the resulting possibility to modify human life at its basic level—to alter human nature—we as Christian people and members of the human race are faced with moral and ethical challenges that both fascinate and terrify. It is no exaggeration to say that we find ourselves today at a radical juncture in human existence, one that will have more far-reaching consequences than any that has preceded it.[1]

---

[1]A slightly modified version of this chapter appeared in *St Vladimir's Theological Quarterly*: John Breck, "Bioethical Challenges in the New Millennium: An Orthodox Response," *St Vladimir's Theological Quarterly* 46, no. 4 (2002): 315–29; and *St Vladimir's Theological Quarterly* 48, no. 4 (2004): 339–53.

Speaking from an evolutionary point of view, scientists are predicting that in the developmental scheme of things, *Homo sapiens*—whom Scripture identifies as Adam, the human person created in the image of God and called to attain the divine likeness, or holiness—is currently drawing near to extinction and is destined to give way to *Homo scientificus*. This is "scientific man," the new creature of the new age, whose existence is not only maintained by technology but also is defined by it. When the term *cyborg* (for cybernetic organism) came into use around 1960, no one expected that within four decades a bionic human would actually exist. Yet recent scientific applications, from pacemakers for the heart to microchips implanted in the brain, have produced precisely that: human beings whose normal biological functioning is enhanced by technological wizardry. Recent experiments with rats and monkeys have proved that brains and electronics can interact in such a way that an animal's activity can be precisely directed by electrodes implanted in the pleasure centers of the brain. Neural implants have already allowed mute patients to communicate via computer and deaf persons to hear. Similar advances in the interlink between the human brain and electronic devices will enable the paralyzed to regain use of their limbs. To some, this represents the fulfillment of the gospel promise that the dumb will speak, the blind will see, and the lame will walk. To others, it means that the line between human and artificial life is perilously thin. While neuroimplants may allow some patients to recover physical movement and others to communicate or to activate thought-controlled limbs, this new technology also poses a potential threat to personal autonomy. If electronics allow us to control, they could also allow us to be controlled, and the question is, By whom and to what end?

Still more radical and potentially more troubling are the new possibilities for modifying genes *in vitro* during the zygote's growth into a human embryo. On the one hand, this could lead to extraordinary and welcome new cures for illnesses and disabilities caused by defective genes. On the other hand, these developments open the way to production of "designer babies," children whose traits are selected by the parents and whose very nature is substantially modified in the interests of a new eugenics.

However accurate the Darwinian or other evolutionary models might be (for example, Harvard paleontologist Stephen Jay Gould's "punctuated equilibrium"), the natural forces behind those models are being superseded by human ingenuity. We are remaking ourselves in an image that reflects both arrogance and desperation. Arrogance, in the assumption that we belong to ourselves rather than to God, and that therefore we have the right to reshape ourselves according to our most appealing fantasies. Desperation, to the degree that the quest for perfect health, longer life, greater physical strength, and a superior IQ stems from a gut-wrenching dread of death and annihilation.

This transformation from man created in the image and likeness of God to man fabricated according to his passions and desires is revolutionary rather than evolutionary. From gene sequencing to human cloning, the first years of this new millennium have been marked by the most rapid and potentially dangerous change in human history. The ethical questions and challenges raised by this transformation are daunting. Will *Homo scientificus* in fact be human? Or, as some have suggested, do we need to speak rather of *Res scientificus*, the human being transmogrified into a technologically sophisticated thing or object?

The Threat of New Diseases

The major bioethical challenges we face today are not all man-made. They don't all result from a human inventiveness that could too easily go awry. Some of the most fearsome challenges concern our response to new outbreaks of disease over which we have little or no control. The ethical issue concerns the way we react to those diseases and how we use available resources in an effort to heal those afflicted by them and to eradicate the diseases wherever possible.

The most obvious is the human immunodeficiency virus (HIV) that has caused millions to suffer and to die from AIDS. As long as the rate of infection is declining in our own country, it is easy to forget that the African continent is facing a horrendous AIDS epidemic, and that Southeast Asia is registering frightening increases in its occurrence. For some Orthodox Christians, it has been easy to ignore the tragedy under the pretext that it is caused primarily by homosexual activity, which could have been avoided. Some Orthodox, and many other Christians, still see AIDS as God's punishment for what they judge to be sexual perversion. In reality, most cases of HIV infection around the world occur through heterosexual activity and other means, such as blood transfusions or transmission from an infected mother to her unborn child. And it needs to be stressed again and again that God does not inflict as punishment epidemics that strike indiscriminately. Nor is there any indication that in his eyes homosexual conduct is any more reprehensible than many commonly accepted heterosexual practices or, for that matter, than other sinful acts such as slander, theft, or child abuse. AIDS is a tragic consequence of viral infection, whatever the means of transmission.

It needs to be recognized for what it is and combated with every appropriate resource at our disposal. Each of us must be concerned by it, if for no other reason than the fact that to one degree or another, each of us is threatened by it, and that threat will only increase in the foreseeable future.

Central Africa is an incubator for incurable diseases of many sorts, and with the ease of modern travel, the spread of those diseases is inevitable. Many diseases, such as staphylococcus, tuberculosis, and other bacterial infections, and viruses, such as HIV, are thriving, and others, once thought eradicated, are making an ominous comeback. Perhaps the most threatening virus—because it is virulent, widespread, and incurable—is the Ebola virus. This deadly infectious agent causes a hemorrhagic fever, with severe external and internal bleeding, and it has already decimated entire villages in parts of Africa. It too knows nothing of geographic boundaries.

One of the most curious and potentially deadly sources of disease, in both humans and animals, is the prion. This is an infectious protein that contains no nucleic acid (DNA or RNA). Although it acts like a virus, it is not one, yet it brings on viral-like symptoms, including loss of motor control, paralysis, dementia, and eventually brain death. Autopsies reveal large vacuoles in the cortex and cerebellum resulting from the prion's tactic of eating away at the brain. In animals, it produces the notorious mad cow disease, whose human equivalent is Creutzfeldt-Jakob disease, together with other potentially fatal syndromes, including FFI (fatal familial insomnia). Whether infectious or hereditary, or both, prion-related diseases are increasingly common and threaten vital links in the food chain, as well as human beings

directly. (In French, the plural term *prions* also signifies the imperative "Let us pray." Prayer may in fact be our best and perhaps
only hope of defending against them.)

Finally, we need to mention the increasing spread of the malady
known as Alzheimer's, a widespread degenerative disease of the
central nervous system. This well-known, if little understood, illness results from the modification of a natural protein that becomes
toxic to the brain. Its symptoms afflict chiefly the elderly and
include, first, loss of memory, then gradual loss of speech, of cognition, and consequently of relationship with the world. It is a terri-
ble and terrifying illness, which makes inexorable progress and
raises grave moral questions regarding appropriate care for victims
who find themselves in its terminal phase. Once a person has irre-
trievably lost contact with other persons and with himself or herself, is it our moral duty to maintain them in a state of cognitive
limbo, especially when they are no longer able to feed and otherwise care for themselves? Or does compassion oblige us to end
through euthansia their tragic condition? While most of us may feel
we know the answer to that question, when it comes to specific
cases, it is not always evident to the medical team or to family members who suffer the overwhelming grief of gradually losing a loved
one to what is little more than a lingering, living death.

Engineering Ourselves

In the introduction, I pointed out that the field of bioethics normally covers issues related to the beginning of life and to its end.
Accordingly, textbooks and collections of articles in the field tend
to focus initially on questions such as the status of the human

embryo, abortion, and medically assisted forms of reproduction. Then they move to the other end of the spectrum, to take up issues such as the definition of death (whether it should be determined by cardiorespiratory failure or by the irreversible cessation of brain functioning in the cortex, the cerebral hemispheres, or the brain stem); euthanasia (the relation between active and passive forms, together with physician-assisted suicide); the debate over medical heroics and palliative care (including the question of withdrawing or withholding food and hydration from dying patients); together with related matters such as burial practices and cremation.

Today, however, other issues have captured the headlines and vastly extended the range of questions that fall under the rubric of bioethics. Foremost among these is the genetic engineering of human beings. Beginning with 2001 (prior to September 11), the crucial issue was manipulation of the human embryo, particularly with a view to harvesting embryonic stem cells. ESCR (embryonic stem cell research) then set the stage for the following year's obsession with human cloning. Cloning involves asexual reproduction by inserting the nucleus of a somatic cell from the person to be cloned into the enucleated ovum of a donor. Where it is successful, this procedure produces an embryo with the usual complement of forty-six chromosomes, all of which are derived from the original somatic cell. The technique, which initially produced the celebrated (and prematurely deceased) ewe named Dolly, was subsequently refined and used to produce at least one human embryo that grew to the six-cell stage. From South Korea and the United States to Argentina and Italy, researchers are racing to perfect the technique, in order to produce embryos *in vitro* for therapeutic purposes. Recent legislation sanctions ESCR in Korea, England, and the Netherlands, and the United States is on the verge of following suit.[2]

However, an important point needs to be made. Something of a false distinction has been made between therapeutic and reproductive cloning. All cloning by its very nature is reproductive, whatever the length of life the new being may enjoy. Thousands of human embryos are at present being created in order to be destroyed. The moral implications are mind-boggling, yet few in government or in the Church have raised their voices in opposition. We all, it seems, have been seduced by false promises of medical panaceas that will result from embryonic stem cell research and cloning. The fact that adult stem cells have proven in many cases to be as effective as their embryonic counterparts has received relatively little press. For in this utilitarian society of ours, we dare not admit that the objects of this manipulation are in fact human lives. Otherwise, we would have to raise serious questions about everything from the profit margins of pharmaceutical companies to the legitimacy of abortion on demand.

These are simply the most visible and passionately debated moral issues of our day. Any survey of bioethical challenges has to consider as well other concerns that have been with us for generations. These would include the breakdown of the nuclear family and its impact on our youth; the increasing levels of violence, particularly handgun violence, in our homes and schools; an

[2]At the beginning of 2005, the U.S. Congress was still debating legislation that would provide government funding for ESCR. In the very near future, embryonic stem cell research will likely be government policy, despite opposition by the Bush administration.

economic system that favors the rich and the strong over the poor and the weak; lingering racism that hampers the social and economic advancement of large segments of our population; the identification of democracy with capitalism in this country that leads Americans to value competition and profitability over justice and the public good; and last, but certainly not least, the problem of addictive behavior, whose symptoms of alcoholism, obesity, bankruptcy, religious fanaticism, and sexual abuse are bioethical issues of the first importance. They concern human behavior, they impact on the growth and well being of human persons, and they demand that hard choices be made in any attempt to ameliorate their effects on personal and social life.

The Quest for Holiness

Listing some of the world's ills as we just have, even when they are cloaked in the euphemism "ethical challenges," can easily make us feel overwhelmed. We read in the newspapers of embryos created to be destroyed, of partial-birth abortions, of our children killing and being killed by other kids on the playground, of widespread corporate crime, of terrorist attacks in our own backyard, which our government responded to with a murderous, preemptive war. We feel helpless to reverse a flood tide of moral deterioration that threatens to wash away our most cherished social and cultural values, including the institution of marriage and the freedom to pray in public.

Perhaps the major moral and spiritual challenge to Orthodox Christians comes less from the realm of medical technology than from the temptation to what could be called "benign apostasy."

This is the pernicious temptation to renounce—in the name of Christianity—values and convictions that give ultimate meaning to our lives, values such as justice, truth, and beauty, and convictions such as those enshrined in the Church's creeds. It is a temptation to which many Christian churches have already succumbed. But benign apostasy threatens the Orthodox as well. It is subtle and insidious, easily excused under the cover of "relevance." Do we really need Holy Tradition, an elaborate liturgy, or even Scripture in this postmodern age? (I remember my first evening in a Protestant seminary back in 1960. The young instructor who spoke to us insisted repeatedly, "We must make the gospel relevant to our people!" I couldn't help wondering then, as I do now, if the point isn't rather to make our people relevant to the gospel.)

The real ethical challenge for us, as it has been for Christians of every age, is to commit ourselves to a quest for holiness, to become holy, as our heavenly Father is holy. Fundamental to Christian faith is its conviction that the human person is called by God to change, to grow in the power of the Holy Spirit from spiritual infancy to spiritual maturity. This involves above all a struggle against what the Holy Fathers term the passions. These include our basest inclinations as well as thoughts and feelings that drive a wedge between ourselves and God, between ourselves and other persons. The passions are not sinful in and of themselves. They are, however, the product of corrupted nature, and as such they incite to sin. Food was intended for nourishment. Passion, when wrongly directed, transforms the natural act of eating into gluttony, represented by Adam's eating of the forbidden fruit. Sexuality was intended for procreation, for participating through intimate and joyful conjugal union in God's work of creating human persons in his image and likeness. Misdirected passion transforms sexuality into a self-centered drive to satisfy lust. An innate longing for God characterizes human nature as it was intended to be. Passion transforms that longing into idolatry, an insatiable desire to worship, serve, and manipulate gods of our own making. Passion turns righteous indignation into anger and condemnation. It turns desire for participation in the glory of God into vainglory, the need to please others and to receive their praise. It distorts a commitment to truth and justice into expressions of anger and a thirst for vengeance.

By obeying the commandments of Christ, by immersing themselves in the cycle of liturgical worship, by devoting themselves to prayer and the constant reading of Scripture, and by joining confession of sins to an ardent quest for mutual forgiveness and reconciliation, Orthodox Christians acknowledge their need for thoroughgoing change and take significant steps to effect such change. The goal of that inner movement, once again, is holiness. Movement toward that goal is impossible without the transforming power and grace of the Holy Spirit, who is the sole source of our sanctification. Insofar as we achieve this goal and allow the Spirit to work that transformation within us, we sanctify both ourselves and the world around us. Thereby we lay the indispensable foundation for any appropriate response we may offer to the critical bioethical and other moral issues that we face in our day-to-day experience.

How do we embark on the pathway to holiness? The first step is to desire it, to allow God to awaken within us a longing to share in his perfection, his glory, his loving compassion. In the language of the Holy Fathers, this means opening ourselves to the divine energies or attributes that penetrate to the depths of the human soul and effect a radical change in our being, which we are wholly incapable of effecting for ourselves. Luther was right: the Christian is in total bondage, yet the Christian is wholly free. We are in bondage to ourselves and our passions, to the fallen inclinations of mind and heart that create the illusion that we are the center of the universe. We are in bondage to our perceived needs and unconscious habits, to our prejudices and self-righteousness. Left on our own, we are in total bondage and without hope. Yet the Christian is also wholly free. We have been liberated from the corrupting powers of sin and death, transferred from the dominion of Satan to the dominion of Christ, and therefore we live no longer in the flesh but in the spirit, the Spirit of God.

God alone can save us; we cannot save ourselves. Salvation, including the gift of holiness, comes to us as a free gift. "Holy things for the holy," the priest intones as he elevates the eucharistic bread before the fraction. And the choir responds, "One is holy, one is the Lord, Jesus Christ, to the glory of God the Father!" We partake of God's holiness, and it is his holiness that works out for us and within us the transformation of soul and body known in patristic tradition as deification, or eternal participation in the life of God himself.

All is gift. Yet there is an essential synergy or cooperation between ourselves and God in the work of salvation. To the extent that we assume our part in that synergy and remain faithful to its ultimate purpose, we are blessed with the power of God's grace that renews our innermost being. And as we ourselves grow toward the holiness of God, we influence other people, even social structures and institutions. Holiness is a *dynamis*, or power. It is a divine energy that brings about change in the world around us, just as it works change in ourselves.

Our Common Priestly Ministry

Practically speaking, is there really any possibility for us as Orthodox Christians to effect real and positive change in a world fraught with such massive ethical challenges? How can our personal quest for holiness impact in any significant way the decisions and actions of those in positions of power, whether in government, in the corporate world, or in the laboratory? Isn't it utopian, or just plain foolish, to think that we can somehow influence persons who are motivated by the lure of scientific discovery, by the promise of effective therapy for heretofore incurable diseases, and above all, by the promise of virtually limitless profits?

Whenever we are faced with challenges or dilemmas that seem overwhelming and irresolvable, it is important to remember the words of the morning prayer attributed to monks of the Optino monastery: "Teach me to treat all that comes to me throughout the day with peace of soul, and with firm conviction that Thy will governs all things." Over the centuries, countless witnesses have affirmed, on the basis of their personal experience, that God's will does indeed govern all things. It is this conviction that has enabled simple, humble people to become courageous martyrs, many of whom have suffered and died in recent years. This conviction too has sustained people of faith whose friends, parents, and children have been murdered in suicide bombings or schoolground massacres. Out of the most pointless tragedy and the most relentless expression of evil, God can bring meaning and work out his purpose. This is as true with bioethical issues as it is with any personal crisis that may overtake us.

How are we to respond in the face of the many ethical challenges that beset us today? The answer is very simply that we are to respond as priests. Priesthood is not reserved to the ordained clergy; it is a fundamental aspect of our vocation as baptized Christians. The First Letter of Peter, which is very likely a baptismal homily, refers to all of us as members of a "holy priesthood," called "to offer spiritual sacrifices to God through Jesus Christ" (2.5). As "a chosen race, a royal priesthood, a holy nation, God's own people," we have been called from darkness into light, in order to declare God's marvelous deeds of salvation (2.9).

A major aspect of that proclamation is to speak God's judgment on every form of sin, including the wanton destruction of innocent human life. Equally important, and equally an element of our common ministry, is intercessory prayer. By our intercession, we hold up to God's light and God's compassion the lives of all those who are victims of the destructive acts of other people, together with the perpetrators themselves. Thus we are called to make a priestly offering of every destroyed embryo, every aborted infant, every child who is subjected to violence and other forms of abuse. Our priestly service also includes offering up to God—with compassion and ongoing care—the disabled members of our society, whom we too easily label "handicapped" and proceed to marginalize. That service includes fervent prayer that begs God's mercy, strength, and peace upon all those who care for the disabled, the sick, and the dying, whether family members or medical professionals. It also entails praying for those who perpetrate crimes of violence, asking God to quicken their conscience, to transform their hearts, and to heal their destructive impulses. We pray for the aggressors as well as for the victims of aggression. And it makes no difference if they are terrorists on the city streets, peddlers of child pornography over the Internet, or practitioners of abortion and euthanasia in our hospitals and clinics.

This kind of priestly service is the responsibility of every baptized Christian, without exception. It is a service by which each of us can offer to God both those who create ethical dilemmas and those who suffer the consequences of those dilemmas. Whether it concerns persons we judge guilty or persons we deem innocent, we hold all of them up before God, asking for his forgiveness and healing grace. In similar fashion, whether the diseases we are facing are caused by sexual misconduct, human indifference, or some uncontrollable plague, we intercede before God on behalf of all those afflicted, seeking his guidance for a just and proper distribution of medical resources. And we do so with the unshakable conviction that God will use our prayers and our concern to work out his will for everyone concerned.

It might sound simplistic or naive to suggest that our most appropriate response to the bioethical and other moral challenges we face today is to pray. Yet even if we were capable of swaying votes in Congress, or banning human cloning, or providing alternatives to abortion and self-inflicted euthanasia, there would be no ultimate purpose to our efforts if they were not undertaken for God's glory and for the fulfillment of his purpose for the world's salvation.

"There's a battle outside," Bob Dylan insisted, "and it's raging." That raging conflict, according to the apostle Paul, is essentially a struggle against principalities and powers, against world rulers of this present darkness, against the spiritual hosts of wickedness in the heavenly places (Eph 6.12). It is a profoundly spiritual struggle, which the Church and its people are called to wage against a culture all too appropriately characterized as a culture of death. Where we can speak and act in such a way as to impede further destruction of human life, and bring healing and peace to those in need, then we must do so with every political, economic, and spiritual resource at our disposal.

Although in many areas the slope has become too slippery for us to reverse a moral decline, we are not without hope. We rely all the more fervently on the power and authority of the God who has created the world and sacrificed his own life for its salvation. We put on the whole armor of God, as the apostle insists, and we "pray at all times in the Spirit, with all prayer and supplication" (Eph 6.18), assured that God hears our prayers and will act on them according to his desires and his intentions.

If we are to respond to these moral challenges in a way that accords with God's will and purpose for ourselves and the world in which we live, we need to assume these challenges with a priestly gesture that submits them entirely into God's hands. We need to hold them in the light of Christ's resurrection—Christ's victory over sin, violence, death, and corruption—with the serene and certain conviction that God's will truly does govern all things.

chapter two

THE COVENANTAL ASPECT
OF CHRISTIAN MARRIAGE

*He who loves a woman, and brings her life to present
realization in his, is able to look in the Thou of her eyes
into a beam of the eternal Thou.*

—Martin Buber, *I and Thou*

Throughout the Western world, secularizing influences are impacting as never before the nuclear family, which historically, in virtually all cultures, has been recognized and protected as the basic unit of social organization. The very institution of marriage is threatened in the United States, Canada, and Western Europe, and a similar trend is increasingly apparent in countries of Eastern Europe. As the relentless march toward the dissolution of the family continues, there inevitably occurs what we are now witnessing: a radical reconceptualizing and restructuring of conjugal relationships, together with a calling into question of the very meaning of marriage.

In this chapter, I would like to offer some reflections on the Orthodox understanding of marriage, particularly as it relates to the covenantal relationship between Christ and the Church. As the term *covenant* implies, this is a relationship of mutual commitment, sealed between God and human persons. A covenant is based on shared trust and responsibility. In Christian terms, marriage is grounded in the same kind of mutual relationship God established with great figures of the Old Testament, such as Abraham, Moses, and King David. Its fullest and perfect expression is the new covenant (or new testament) promised in the prophecy of Jeremiah (31.31–34) and fulfilled in the relationship of mutual service and love between Christ and his body, the Church (Eph 5.21–33).

These reflections offer neither a formal analysis of marriage nor an exhaustive review of possible remedies for the malaise that afflicts it today. I make these remarks simply as a way to refocus our attention and concern on the spiritual and sacramental aspects of conjugal life as they are revealed to us in Holy Scripture and in Church tradition.

As with all things Orthodox, it is essential that we strive for balance. In this case, the needed balance is between, on the one hand, acknowledgment of certain realities concerning gender and sexuality, both heterosexual and homosexual, and on the other hand, affirmation of the Church's traditional stance regarding sexual activity in general and conjugal relations in particular. As Orthodox Christians, we are called today to preserve traditional values, especially in the realm of sexuality, and to do so in the face of tremendous secularizing pressures. This is not, or should not be, because we reject sexual expression on puritanical grounds or recoil from same-sex unions out of homophobic revulsion. It is because the Church recognizes that intimate sexual relations are endowed by God with unitive, sacramental, and procreative potential that can be realized only in a healthy and holy way within the context of a monogamous, heterosexual, blessed, conjugal union. In what follows, I would like to discuss each of these terms and to explain the reason for the Church's traditional view regarding the nature and meaning of the covenantal marriage bond.

Reconceptualizing Sex, Gender, and Marriage

To set the stage for these reflections, let me begin with some vignettes that illustrate the complexity of the issue. Then I would like to suggest possible responses to some of the challenges suggested by these vignettes, responses that have taken shape in my own pastoral experience.

A weekly news magazine recently ran an article with an all too familiar theme. Teenagers were asked why the rate of cohabitation between unmarried boys and girls has increased so greatly in the past decade or so. For some, it was a matter of "being in love," yet being equally wary of long-term commitment. For others, it was because "everybody else is doing it." Like smoking among kids a generation ago, cohabitation without the benefit of marriage has today become something of a status symbol. Its often harmful effect, however, is a certain depersonalization in the sexual and emotional relationship of the couple, precisely because genuine commitment—which implies appropriate conjugal chastity and ascetic struggle to put first the needs of the spouse— is so often missing. The depersonalization of sex, however, is hardly limited to couples who live together with no long-term commitment. The article also mentions the remarks of a girl who was entering her last year in high school. When she was asked about the lack of emotional nurturing that accompanies casual sex, she replied, "I have my friends for my emotional needs, so I don't need that from the guy I'm having sex with." As one psychologist points out, "Young people are learning to view each other as interchangeable sex objects." And she adds, almost rhetorically, "How can they ever be developmentally ready for real-life relationships?"

A short time ago, my wife spoke to me about a situation that's far more prevalent than I had realized. Increasing numbers of America's children, beginning in middle school, are engaging in oral sex, often in groups. When asked about it, they tend to deny that they are "having sex" at all. They have, it seems, been persuaded by the arguments of a former occupant of the White House that anything short of—or other than—completed coitus does not qualify as sex. One young girl commented about the intimacy she shared with her boyfriend, "Well, it's just like kissing any other part of the body." To which my wife replied, "No it's not, honey!"

A fellow whom I didn't know phoned last fall and asked whether I as an Orthodox priest would marry him and his girlfriend. This would be, he added, his fourth marriage. When I refused, he didn't wait for an explanation. He just hung up.

A while back, I picked up a video at our local Pick-a-Flick. It was to be a lazy diversion on a Friday evening when my wife and I were too tired to do anything more constructive. The film featured, and was produced by, a popular, highly paid actress who had appeared in a couple of innocent comedies the year before. Halfway into it, there was a scene that depicted her and her costar engaged in the most graphic intercourse imaginable. The scene was gratuitous; it had no relevance to the rest of the film whatsoever. I found the minuscule R on the cover's rating chart, which I hadn't bothered to look for in the video store. It brought home the point that much of what today is rated merely PG-13 would have carried a large X when I was in school. But then, that was a long time ago.

On May 18, 2004, the state of Massachusetts joined the Netherlands, Belgium, the city of San Francisco, and several Canadian provinces in offering marriage licenses to couples of the same gender. Then, in the early summer of 2005, the Canadian parliament passed legislation that permits throughout the provinces marriage between two men or two women. Spain and other countries, including our own, are not far behind. *Same-sex marriage* is no longer an oxymoron. It has become enshrined in the rule of law.

Such is today's reality: couples living together in what we used to call concubinage; young teenagers engaged in sexual activity their parents hardly have the vocabulary to describe; serial divorce as an increasingly normal aspect of our social order; blatant, in-your-face pornography in everything from mail-order catalogs to video entertainment, cable television, and the Internet; and marriage redefined so as to include same-sex coupling. As Fr Thomas Hopko[1] began pointing out many years ago, "sex and gender" is without question the chief theological and pastoral issue of our day.

Before I go any further, let me say a word about what I feel needs to be our response to at least some of these situations I've just noted.

[1]Former Dean and Professor of Dogmatic Theology Emeritus at St Vladimir's Seminary.

It would be easy for us as Orthodox Christians to condemn outright this kind of behavior on the part of young and not-so-young members of our society. We could react with a polemic that invokes biblical passages against everything from divorce to fornication to homosexuality. Or we could quietly resign ourselves to the realities of this fallen world, hoping against hope that our own children will somehow be insulated from it all. Neither approach is helpful; neither approach speaks to the real needs of our adolescents.

However we may judge various expressions of sexual behavior today, it is imperative that we, as members of the body of Christ, hear our young people, attempt to understand their reasoning, and speak to it and to them as directly, yet compassionately and lovingly, as we can. At the same time, we need to provide them with serious, balanced, and healthy education on the subject of sexuality—from life-giving procreation to death-dealing AIDS—and to do so within our homes as well as in our parish churches.

With regard to unmarried couples living together, we need to hear the reluctance of many people to enter into a legal marriage today, when the divorce rate hovers near 50 percent and prenuptial agreements can't eliminate either the heartache or the red tape involved in a divorce settlement. If they seem willfully to ignore what we consider to be Christian values related to married life, it's often because we ourselves have failed to offer them an acceptable model of appropriate and ultimately fulfilling conjugal relationships. Then again, if our children's attitude toward sexuality is distressingly casual, devoid of real depth and commitment, it's largely because we have allowed our cultural milieu to cheapen sex and to strip it of genuine mystery. If they act out sexually in ways that older generations might find shockingly salacious, it is chiefly due to a failure on our part to convey certain truths: the truth that each human person is of infinite value and therefore deserves unconditional respect, including respect for bodily intimacy; or the truth that the joy, the beauty, and the ultimate purpose of authentic marriage are given by God as foretastes of life in the kingdom of heaven.

Our children's behavior, and the dissolution of sexual morality in general, reflects as much on us as it does on them. Rather than blame, condemn, and reject them and their behavior, we need to listen, to teach, to guide, to bless, and to forgive. We need to understand—even when we cannot approve—their motivations, their fears, and their longings. Above all, we need to rediscover the essence of Christian marriage, for ourselves as much as for them, and allow it to transform our own conjugal relationships into a living image or icon of the love and mutual self-offering that unite Christ and the Church in a "great mystery" (Eph 5.32).

Much of the same approach is needed with regard to same-sex unions, whether or not they are granted the legal status of marriage. Again, it would be easy for us as Orthodox Christians to condemn homosexuality and same-sex coupling without attempting to understand the motivations of the persons involved or the factors that underlie their behavior. Scripture unambiguously condemns homosexual acts, and the apostle Paul adds that those who commit such acts "will not inherit the kingdom of God." To those thus condemned, however, he adds as well those who are prone to verbal abuse (*loidoroi*), drunkards (*methusoi*), and even the greedy (*pleonektai*) (1 Cor 6.9–10). The point is not that these are acceptable behaviors and that Paul was simply wrong. The point is that we now know that behind many behaviors recognized in antiquity as inherently sinful, there are often unconscious motivations and impulses that condition those behaviors. They are not necessarily, as everyone until recently assumed them to be, expressions of the will acting in unrestrained freedom. Drunkenness we now rightly identify as alcoholism, an addiction properly characterized as a disease. And all of us, from time to time, succumb to verbal abuse and greed.

This is not to minimize these sins. It is to say rather that their inclusion in St Paul's list needs to be understood in its cultural, historical, and even medical contexts. The same is true with homosexuality. Until recently, that too was thought to be an expression of free will. Today, we know that there is a "homosexual orientation" distinct from particular acts. Whether that orientation is due to nature or nurture, to genes or to the environment, is still an open question. However it may be resolved, we should still attempt to understand the feelings and behaviors that gays and lesbians experience. This does not mean that we must approve homosexual acts. To the contrary, despite self-justifying protestations from the gay community, pastoral experience, coupled with the genetic and environmental factors involved in homosexuality, lead many of us to the conviction that there is something unhealthy, dysfunctional, or disordered in the homosexual condition itself, and that therefore it is potentially destructive when it issues in sexual activity. Nevertheless, it is imperative that we condemn the sin and not the sinner, particularly where the person desires either to change their sexual orientation, insofar as that might be possible, or to accept the rigors of chastity.

Can the Orthodox Church, then, ever bless gay marriage or same-sex unions? The answer must surely be no. Once again, this is not, or should not be, a puritanical or homophobic reaction against what many people consider to be aberrant and repulsive behavior. Rather, it is because there is a better way in terms of both spiritual and physical well being. That better way might well require that persons with marked homosexual tendencies accept a lifelong struggle to remain chaste, together with sincere repentance when and if they fall. In this regard, however, they are no different from unmarried heterosexual men and women, who likewise have to struggle against sexual desires and temptations in order to remain chaste. Certainly this is an unpopular stance, one that is considered thoroughly outmoded even by many of our faithful. Nonetheless, the Church's monastic tradition long ago confirmed the spiritual and physiological value of chastity, the virtue of refraining from sexual activity. Not all of us are called to monasticism, many people will reply, and they are right. This does not alter the fact, however, that the body's sexual energy can be redirected from a lustful quest for sexual gratification toward a deep and sanctifying expression of charity. This redirection is essential for creating an appropriate chastity within marriage, one based not on sexual abstinence but on mutual love and respect, together with ongoing concern for the other's needs and desires. Particularly for those who are called to a life of celibacy, the *erōs* of the flesh can and should be progressively transformed into a "divine *erōs*," expressed as an insatiable longing for ultimate union with the God of love.

This said, it is clear that same-sex unions are with us, and they are here to stay. Our local Greek church recently published its annual bulletin, replete with photos of parish couples, husbands and wives smiling broadly at the camera. There in the midst of them is a photo of two smiling young men, who obviously form their own couple. I asked the priest how he dealt with the situation pastorally. Like so many of our priests today, he finds himself in a quandary. For better or for worse (more likely the latter), he has adopted a "don't ask, don't tell" policy. Many of our communities are wrestling with similar situations. Sometimes homosexual couples attend services but refrain from communion. Others come to communion but refrain from confession. In both cases, we are confronted with a serious pastoral issue.

Nevertheless, we have to ask the following question: Is homosexuality, especially as expressed by a stable couple who have committed themselves to each other, a serious enough sin—or a destructive enough influence in parish life—to warrant excommunicating them? We don't excommunicate those who fall into St Paul's category of the greedy, particularly when the parish budget depends on their sizeable contributions. Nor do most of us excommunicate drunkards, that is, alcoholics, even when they give in repeatedly to the bottle. We recognize that communion in the Body and Blood of Christ is offered to us "for the healing of soul and body." What indeed is an appropriate pastoral approach to same-sex couples who participate actively in parish life?

Without attempting to resolve the issue here, we can say at least the following. It seems appropriate to make a distinction between same-sex unions and same-sex marriage. Regarding the former, same-sex unions are now a given in many Western societies, including our own. In their defense is the fact that they protect against legal and social injustices. They also provide an alternative to the rampant promiscuity that has led to so much suffering and death in this age of AIDS. Also, since such couples may legally adopt children, granting social and legal recognition to their union would offer some stability and protection to those children who might otherwise go without.

Despite these points, however, it seems equally clear that the Church should not formally bless such unions. Insofar as they involve active homosexual relations, they are based on a relationship we can view only as sinful and unhealthy. That relationship, by the way, may be particularly unhealthy when such couples adopt children or bring them into the world via artificial insemination. A popular book written some years ago for grammar school children, *Heather Has Two Mommies*, paints a favorable picture of the life of a young girl who is the child of a lesbian couple. Heather may have two mommies, but there is no doubt she would be better off, all other things being equal, if she had a mommy and a daddy. This is a truth inscribed in human nature itself, and it needs to be recognized and defended accordingly.

All the more firmly, we must categorically reject growing pressures toward universal acceptance of same-sex marriages. The term *marriage* itself needs to be retained, preserved, and protected to signify exclusively the union of one man and one woman, joined in a formal bond characterized by faithfulness and permanence. This definition, as we shall see, is inadequate with regard to Christian marriage. But even in secular usage, the term marriage needs to retain its conventional definition. This is necessary to preserve the social, psychological, and spiritual roles of the traditional nuclear family, which is based on gender complementarity between husband and wife. It is also necessary to preserve the possibility for Christians, Jews, and other believers to define the conditions of marriage according to their own convictions.

Same-sex marriage is, and always will be, an oxymoron. Despite pressures for political correctness in this environment of moral relativism, the term marriage must be preserved to designate the unique union between a man and a woman that God himself has established, in order to serve his purposes for the propagation of life and the salvation of us all. Whether or not this will necessitate a constitutional amendment, it requires that we as Christian people rediscover and give new life to our traditional concept of marriage. More important than any piece of legislation is the witness we can offer to the world around us. For that witness to be effective, however, we need to embody in our families the commitment and responsibility, the faithfulness and love, that God calls for in the covenantal and sacramental bond of conjugal union.

The Reason for Marriage

In his still-valuable ethical treatise titled *The Destiny of Man*, Nicholas Berdyaev declares that "love is the ontological basis of the marriage union." And, he continues, "The meaning and purpose of the union between man and woman is to be found not in the continuation of the species or in its social import but in personality [personhood] in its striving for the completeness and fullness of life and its longing for eternity."[2]

[2]Nicholas Berdyaev, *The Destiny of Man* (New York: Harper and Brothers, 1960), 239–40.

With these words, Berdyaev provides a profoundly Orthodox answer to a question long debated in Roman Catholic and Protestant circles. There the question as to the basic meaning and end of marriage has led to a certain polarization. Catholic theology has tended to argue that marriage is justified primarily, if not exclusively, by creating the appropriate framework for procreation. Directly or indirectly, this emphasis led to a magisterial ban on contraception and, it could be argued, to the mandatory celibacy of priests. Protestants, on the other hand, have tended to stress the unitive value of marriage, its capacity to unite husband and wife in an affectionate bond that serves to strengthen mutual commitment between the spouses and thereby strengthen family integrity. In this perspective, procreation is important, but it is not primary. As evidence, Protestant ethicists point to the fact that many couples are incapable of procreating (because of age, for example, or sterility), yet their marriage can be blessed by the Church, and their conjugal union is in no way diminished.

As Berdyaev's remarks indicate, Orthodoxy considers both the unitive and the procreative aspects of marriage to be important. Yet it finds the ultimate reason for conjugal union in a higher truth. Husband and wife are joined in marriage to participate in a self-giving love of transcendent origin. That love, which creates mutual desire as it brings forth a new reality of "one flesh," finds its most sublime expression in the longing the couple shares for eternal life in communion with the Holy Trinity. In addition to procreation and committed union, Orthodoxy understands the ultimate purpose and meaning of marriage to be *soteriological*: through it, husband and wife are called and enabled to work out their mutual salvation. To grasp the mystery of one-flesh union as

God intended it, therefore, we need to approach it from the perspective of the Church's theology, rather than, for example, from that of the medieval conception of romantic love or the modern psychotherapeutic notion of love as a means for self-fulfillment.

A more appropriate model for expressing the *mysterion*, or sacramental quality, of conjugal love is provided by Martin Buber's profound insights into the human person expressed as the relationship between I and Thou. In marriage, he affirms, two I's, man and woman, enter into the transcendent world of Thou, to perceive in each other unique value and meaning. Each becomes for the other a veritable symbol, a reality that brings together the temporal and the eternal. Yet because they dwell in the sphere of time and space, each spouse tends to lapse into an objectivity characterized as the sphere or world of It. Conjugal love in all its complexity, which encompasses every aspect of the couple's being, has as its basic function to lead the objective He and She back to a relationship of I-Thou.[3]

Anglican theologian Derrick Bailey expresses this theme in a passage of his book *The Mystery of Love and Marriage* that underscores the difference in perspective between an onlooker and the couple who are united as lover and the beloved. "To the onlooker," he says, "the beloved belongs to the world of It, and she is accordingly assessed by conventional standards at her 'face value.' But to the lover she is Thou: through the relational event of falling in love, with its vision of perfection, he has seen her, not as she is, but as she may become by the grace of God—and he cannot forget what he has seen. She has been revealed as God made

---

[3]Martin Buber, *I and Thou*, 2nd ed. (New York: Scribner's, 1958).

her to be and wills her to become, and she is loved both as she is and as grace may remake her."[4]

Perhaps the most important way to maintain conjugal faithfulness is to love the other precisely as he or she truly is, yet also as grace may remake them. To encounter the other on their own terms, as God has created them and has willed them to become, is to engage in a unique meeting with the other. It is to root the marriage relationship in all the harsh reality of daily life and struggle. Yet at the same time, it is to constantly transcend that reality, to discover in the other the beauty and perfection of the person, who bears the divine image and likeness. While they enjoy all the fruits and joys of erotic love, the couple thereby grows together in a deeper *erōs*, experienced as a hunger for eternal union with God.

Sexual relations, then, are not to be set aside and are certainly not to be despised as a concession to the fleshly passions. They are a God-given means by which the couple can know each other with the greatest possible intimacy and fullness. By means of that carnal knowledge, they can enter into communion through each other with God, who is the object of their deepest and most sublime longing.

Characteristics of Christian Marriage

Earlier, I qualified Christian marriage with four adjectives: monogamous, heterosexual, blessed, and conjugal. Each of these

---

[4]Derrick Sherwin Bailey, *The Mystery of Love and Marriage* (New York: Harper and Row, 1952), 16.

is critical for establishing the unique covenantal bond between husband and wife that reflects the relationship of sacrificial love between Christ and the Church.

These adjectives describe the content and limits of the union assumed by a Christian couple through the sacrament of marriage, understood in its broadest sense. Like the liturgical offices of baptism and chrismation, the marriage service is one of initiation. It introduces the couple into a new reality, a new mode of being, as it makes of them a new creation of one flesh. The sacramental aspect of that new creation is not limited to the liturgical service but should continue and grow throughout the lifetime of the persons concerned. Just as one's entire life consists of an ongoing renewal of baptismal grace through the power of the Holy Spirit, so in marriage there should be a continual deepening and perfecting of the grace conferred through the Church's blessing at the time of the wedding service.

The term marriage, therefore, refers to a lifelong venture of faithful and responsible commitment to the welfare and salvation of the other, the spouse. Yet it is more than a union between two people. Christian marriage is an icon of the loving relationship between Christ and his entire body, the universal Church. It finds its power and its ultimate purpose through participation in that relationship. Marriage is thus essentially an *ecclesial* reality. Intensely personal on the level of sexual and other expressions of intimacy, it is profoundly communal insofar as the couple responds to the call to make of their relationship an authentic covenant: a bond between persons, yet a bond that unites them with God and with the entire *ecclesia*, the universal communion of saints, both living and departed.

Elsewhere I have attempted to spell out the covenantal nature of Christian marriage, and I don't want to repeat that reflection here.[5] It's enough to recall God's covenantal bond with his people Israel, sealed with Adam, Abraham, Moses, David, and the prophets. "In each case," I note, "the two parties of the covenantal bond commit themselves to unconditional faithfulness toward the fulfillment of a pledge or promise that will last forever." The key terms here are "unconditional faithfulness" and "forever." This does not mean that the bond cannot be ruptured and the covenantal relationship ended. Israel repeatedly betrays its commitment to the Lord. That commitment is restored and renewed only by means of repentance, to which God responds with forgiveness. The covenantal bond of marriage can also be broken, most visibly through divorce. Yet like Israel's relationship with Yahweh, the covenant of marriage can also be effectively voided by adultery, rebellion, or mere indifference. Where infidelity, abuse, or neglect characterize relations between spouses, the sacramental aspect of their union is vitiated and the specifically covenantal dimension of their relationship is lost, broken. Yet it too can be restored by genuine repentance coupled with willing forgiveness.

Monogamous. If Christian marriage is necessarily monogamous, it is precisely because of the couple's relationship with God. As the prophets of Israel repeatedly affirm, the Lord is a jealous God. His love for his people is complete and without limit. It extends to all of humanity and to all of creation. Yet that love also focuses uniquely on every individual. Each one of us becomes in God's

[5]John Breck, *The Sacred Gift of Life: Orthodox Christianity and Bioethics* (Crestwood, NY: St Vladimir's Seminary Press, 2000), 60–69.

eyes his unique beloved, his "only begotten" child. As God commits himself to us, so Christian marriage requires that two persons, a man and a woman, commit themselves, totally and without compromise, both to each other and to God. Their loving commitment too is exclusive, unique, and complete. Only as such can it bear witness to the boundless and unique love of Christ for his Church.

To be loved is a basic human need, and especially to be loved by someone in particular. Equally basic is the need to love another, to direct both affective and sexual energy toward a specific person—the beloved—who calls forth our absolute trust and undivided devotion. It is precisely the uniqueness of the relationship that enables that person, and that person alone, to become for me a Thou, so that we might share together and fill for each other the most significant times and spaces of our daily existence.

The monogamous character of Christian marriage therefore excludes not only polygamy but also adultery, and that in all its forms, including fantasies directed toward someone other than the spouse. To look at another with lust, Jesus declared, is tantamount to committing adultery with that person. This is a hard saying, especially for our sex-saturated society. But it is a crucial one, in that it calls us repeatedly to repentance and a refocusing of our care and our affection on the person who shares the covenantal bond with us.

Monogamy allows for mutual care, nurture, and growth, while it opens before the couple a pathway that leads beyond the flesh and into the realm of spirit. This is simply not possible with casual partners taken in serial or simultaneous relationships, in which the primary motivation is sexual gratification. There the other person is inevitably objectified. In Buber's language, they are rendered a He or a She in a world of It. The chief virtue of monogamy is that it allows the time to know the beloved in all the complex and beautiful mystery of his or her being. To acquire this kind of knowledge requires a lifetime, since persons change and grow every day. And it can last beyond a lifetime, when the living spouse maintains with the deceased loved one a relation of ongoing communion, a relation of I and Thou. Although the Church blesses second marriages, it also affirms that conjugal union possesses a sacramental—which is to say eternal—quality. If the couple so desires it, and if through their mutual devotion and faithful commitment they strive to attain it, their covenantal, sacramental union can endure and grow beyond death and into eternity.

Heterosexual. In the second place, Christian marriage is necessarily heterosexual. Until very recently, the notion that any marriage can be only heterosexual was accepted as axiomatic in virtually every major world culture. In an extraordinarily brief period of time, the popular attitude toward homosexuality has shifted from universal rejection to near universal acceptance. This is due in part to recognition that a homosexual orientation does in fact exist. According to frequently cited statistics, it is an orientation that can be changed in fewer than 40 percent of the cases in which such change is desired.[6]

---

[6]Statistics regarding successful attempts to change a homosexual orientation vary widely. This is due in part to the taboo surrounding the subject, but also to how treatment is applied and healing is measured. Depending on the source, we read that anywhere from 25 percent to 65 percent of those who seek medical or psychological therapy achieve their goal. See John F. Harvey, *The Truth about Homosexuality* (San Francisco: Ignatius, 1996), for a

More significant, though, is the prevailing atmosphere in Western societies that sets personal rights and individual freedom above notions of social responsibility. Sexual acts committed between consenting adults, the argument goes, should remain private, whatever their nature. Any suggestion that private acts may have public consequences is brushed aside as politically incorrect and fundamentally intrusive.

Then again, the "gay agenda" has been championed by much of the media, including such influential forums as prime-time television and *Newsweek* magazine. In our schools and universities, this has reached the point where First Amendment rights are seriously jeopardized. It's increasingly difficult, if not downright dangerous, to say anything at all in public that questions the morality of sexual activity between same-sex partners. Before long, we may expect to see laws passed that will penalize not only negative comments but mere references to biblical passages that condemn homosexuality. Then it will be impossible to take a public stand against same-sex unions or marriages, because such arguments will be classed as "hate speech." As a result, Christians, Jews, and Muslims who preach against such unions, even within their religious communities, will be liable to prosecution.

On the other hand, it is important for us as Orthodox to place the matter in perspective. Homosexuality may well be condemned by Scripture and the Church's moral tradition. It may be unhealthy

detailed discussion by a Roman Catholic priest and therapist who has had significant success in helping persons change from a homosexual to a heterosexual orientation; and Jeffrey Satinover, M.D., *Homosexuality and the Politics of Truth* (Grand Rapids, MI: Baker, 1996), esp. 168–209.

and even life-threatening when there is a possibility of HIV or other sexually transmitted infection.[7] Homosexual acts may be distasteful, even repulsive, to those who do not share those proclivities. They may well involve a misuse of our genitalia and represent a travesty of God-intended sexual relations. But homosexuality, even when acted out, is hardly the worst of sins. More reprehensible, certainly, are other offenses that directly threaten both the social welfare and the Church's integrity, offenses such as corporate corruption, child abuse, or bishops willy-nilly excommunicating each other. These sins impact directly, and in the most serious way, on the life and welfare of large numbers of persons whose trust has been betrayed. Consequently, they deserve our attention at least as much as, if not more than, homosexual acting out, particularly when the latter involves two people who engage in those acts freely within a committed relationship.

Yet it is of the essential nature of marriage that it be and remain heterosexual, a union of one man and one woman. Gender complementarity is necessary for procreation, at least in the conventional sense and for the foreseeable future.[8] And however significant the unitive value of conjugal life may be, the basic reason for sexuality and marriage remains the God-given invitation to "multiply and fill the earth." It is precisely the heterosexual

---

[7]It is important to note that HIV is also transmitted through heterosexual activity, which is the most common mode, for example, throughout Africa.

[8]Embryologists are talking today about the feasibility of parthenogenic reproduction, a sort of "virgin birth," by which an ovum is stimulated *in vitro* to begin mitosis and embryonic development without being fertilized by a male gamete. This raises ethical issues of huge proportions, which we will discuss in the next chapter.

quality of marriage that enables the couple to procreate, to participate in God's ongoing work of creating persons who bear his divine image.

Blessed. The third adjective that qualifies authentic marriage is the one that makes it specifically Christian. A conjugal union is to be blessed by God through the public, sacramental ritual that constitutes the wedding ceremony. That blessing bestows on the couple the grace that creates of their union a genuine vocation, a divine calling, whose basic task is to "be fruitful and multiply" (Gen 1.28). As a blessed reality, marriage unites the couple in a new and unique way to the covenant that God establishes with his faithful people. It inserts them into the flow of salvation history, which begins with the patriarchs and culminates in the life of the Church. Therefore, the great prayer of the Orthodox crowning service repeatedly asks God to bless them, as he blessed Abraham and Sarah, Isaac and Rebecca, Joachim and Anna, Zechariah and Elisabeth:

> "Bless," "preserve," and "remember them, O Lord, as You remembered Enoch, Shem and Elijah. Remember them, O Lord our God, as You remembered Your forty holy martyrs, sending down upon them crowns from heaven."

This blessing is effectively symbolized by the wedding crowns, which in the Russian tradition are both ornate and heavy. They represent both the glory of the newly formed couple and the ascetic struggle that lies ahead of them. God's blessing, expressed through the ritual crowning, involves the spouses in a pilgrimage that joins them, in both struggle and victory, with patriarchs and prophets of the Old Covenant, and with apostles and martyrs of the New. This double emphasis is also reflected in childbearing. The mother's participation in God's creative handiwork involves both suffering and joy. "When a woman is in travail," Jesus declares, "she has sorrow, because her hour has come; but when she is delivered of the child, she no longer remembers the anguish, for joy that a child is born into the world" (Jn 16.21). Assuming the weighty crowns of conjugal union, husband and wife together struggle and labor once "the hour has come." Specifically, the woman's hour of delivery becomes a symbol of the hour of Christ's passion. Yet through both—her anguish and his—new life is brought forth. As Christ's death issued in resurrection, so the woman's travail issues in new birth. Accordingly, the wedding crowns witness to God's promise that for those who remain faithful to his covenant, sealed by his blessing bestowed through the marriage ceremony, crowns of martyrdom will one day be transformed into crowns of victory and joy.

Conjugal. Finally, Christian marriage is truly conjugal. This should be a tautology. But in today's atmosphere of serial divorce and minimal commitment, it needs to be affirmed. In a Christian perspective, marriage is truly conjugal only insofar as it represents a new creation of one flesh, which images the union in perfect love and devotion between Christ and his Church.

Christian marriage, then, is utterly different from secular unions, including those nominally sealed by a church service. The primary and essential component of a genuinely Christian marriage is the commitment on the part of each spouse to love, forgive, embrace, and nurture the other as Christ loves, forgives, embraces, and nurtures all those who are baptized into his body. The Holy Fathers repeatedly invoke nuptial imagery to describe the relationship between Christ and the soul. They frequently use the language of the biblical Song of Songs to speak of the passionate, truly erotic quality of love that unites the soul to Christ, as a bride is united to her beloved. If this imagery is acceptable to our spiritual elders, it is because Holy Tradition itself so highly values the true purpose and meaning of marriage: to serve as a living icon of divine *erōs*, divine love.

Does Christian Marriage Have a Future?

The institution of marriage, in conventional terms, is so threatened today that its future is clearly in jeopardy. But this fact merely underscores the need within God's world for authentic marriages that both witness to God's covenantal love and provide the matrix in which that love can work out salvation, both for the spouses and for their children.

In the face of all of the challenges thrown up today against the institution of marriage, our vocation as Christian people is clear. It is to rediscover and relive within our conjugal unions a depth of devotion, commitment, faithfulness, and love that heals and transforms the profound loneliness that threatens the lives of each of us in a hostile and meaningless world. It is to rediscover the truth that marriage is most firmly grounded in *friendship*—a delight in the other person, a joy in their presence, a respect for their feelings and integrity, and a devotion so pure and boundless that we are willing to die for that person. If the divorce rate is what it is, if domestic violence and neglect are so common in this society, it is largely because the spouses have never discovered in each other a real friend—a unique confidant, a source of intellectual stimulation and spiritual enlightenment, a person with whom they can share laughter, tears, and mutual delights.

Christian marriage certainly has a future, and a promising one as well, to the degree that believing couples assume their conjugal union as a spiritual vocation that is given, blessed, and fulfilled by God. And it will be a union not only of obligation and sacrifice but also of devotion and joy insofar as they take to heart a simple bit of popular wisdom each of us should tape to our refrigerator door: happiness is being married to your best friend.

chapter three

THE USE AND ABUSE
OF HUMAN EMBRYOS

It is a curious thing to observe the excitement many geneticists express over the mere prospect of increasing man's intelligence (they express no desire whatsoever for increasing man's humility). Insufficient intelligence, however, has never been a serious human problem. In fact, many of our problems are associated with intelligence that is separated and isolated from its saving graces of humility, understanding, and wisdom.

—Donald DeMarco, in *The Concentration Can*

Before I formed you in the womb I knew you, and before you were born I consecrated you; I appointed you a prophet to the nations.

—Jeremiah 1.5

Behold, you will conceive in your womb and bear a son, and you shall call his name Jesus.

—Luke 1.31

From the perspective of Orthodox Christianity, all research on human subjects—including embryonic stem cell research (ESCR) and cloning—should be guided and limited by the Christian understanding of the human person as created in the image of God.[1] We can understand the Church's attitude regarding the beginning of human life, and consequently the implications of ESCR and cloning, only on the basis of theology. God alone establishes meaning and purpose in human existence. Therefore, it is only God who provides the moral framework by which we can make judgments regarding medical technology and the manipulation and treatment of human persons.[2]

In today's secular, postmodern, and highly pluralistic world, this kind of affirmation sounds sectarian and retrograde, if not absurd. How can we as Christians impose our standards of moral conduct on a society that has abandoned those standards in favor of a philosophical relativism that rejects the very existence of absolute values and truths? Indeed, how can we even speak of a Christian perspective regarding moral judgments when Christians of various confessional backgrounds hold very different opinions as to how we are to interpret Scripture and early Church tradition, and to how we should apply our interpretations in specific cases?

---

[1] I wish to express my very sincere thanks to Dr Gayle Woloschak of the Feinberg School of Medicine, Northwestern University, and to Dr Terry Orr-Weaver of the Massachusetts Institute of Technology, for comments and criticisms they have offered on this subject and for scientific materials they have provided for me. All interpretations and conclusions drawn here are, of course, my own and should not be taken to reflect their opinions or positions on the questions raised.

[2] Note: all terms in boldface appear in the glossary at the end of this chapter.

Given this diversity of perspectives, we as Orthodox Christians can only bear witness to what we know and hold to be true. This means that we turn to Holy Tradition, with the conviction that God has revealed his will, and continues to do so, in and through those traditional sources that serve as the ground of our faith: the Old and New Testaments, early patristic teachings, the Church's liturgy, and others. In other words, in this postmodern world, we need to hold, with unwavering conviction and determination, to "the faith once and for all [*tē hapax*] delivered to the saints" (Jude 3).

Such a commitment may sound self-evident. The term postmodern, after all, originally signified the abandoning of modernist trends—in art, literature, and culture in general—to return to more traditional values. In recent years, however, the term's meaning has shifted, so that now, in popular usage, postmodernism signifies something more akin to relativism. It implies, basically, a rejection of absolute and objective values and truths, in the belief that all subjective interpretations of what is good and true are of equal standing. One person's notion of what is right or appropriate in any given situation is as valid as any other's, whatever that notion may be. If, in my opinion, human life only really begins at birth, then I am free to dispose of fetuses as I please, with no moral consequences. Your conviction that life is sacred from conception may be important for you, but you have no right to impose that conviction on me.

The same holds for our treatment of those who are disabled or terminally ill. If I feel they would be better off dead, then I have no moral qualms about euthanizing them. If I can persuade the public and the courts to agree with me, then my relativistic perspective becomes enshrined in law. The result is legislation such as *Roe v. Wade,* which sanctions unrestricted abortion, and Oregon's *Measure 16,* which authorizes physician-assisted suicide. Both of these, popular as they are in today's culture of death, fly in the face of traditional perspectives on the sanctity of life.

Our responsibility before God and neighbor in this postmodern world is, nevertheless, to preserve and to proclaim precisely "the faith once and for all delivered to the saints." The chief ethical question that arises for us is just how we apply the givens of that faith in specific situations that involve the beginning and end of human life.

"God alone is good," Jesus affirms. This means that God is the source of all goodness and that it is he who offers us the criteria by which goodness is judged. Without God, Dostoevsky declared, anything is permissible. Without God, ethics are merely utilitarian. What is good is measured by expediency rather than by its conformity to absolute, immutable truths—that is, by the degree to which it reflects divine perfection. From a utilitarian point of view, the good is determined by its usefulness, and particularly by its capacity to provide the greatest amount of pleasure and happiness to the greatest number of people. On a practical level, utilitarian determination of the good or useful is strongly influenced by economic interests. In the field of medical technology, biotech companies and the pharmaceuticals industry wield extraordinary power in the setting of policies that concern human life at its fundamental level, policies such as the use of embryonic stem cells and fetal tissue in the development of new therapies. All too often, the moral implications of this research are brushed aside not only in the interests of scientific knowledge but also because those therapies are potentially so lucrative. In such a world, what is ethically permissible tends to be whatever promises the most success in providing those therapies and the profits associated with them.

When the laws of the marketplace govern medical care and medical research, as they do in the United States, the potential for innovative therapies is matched by the potential for abuse. During the past few years, secular voices in the medical and pharmaceuticals fields, together with much of the media, have tried to convince us that the human embryo, especially in the earliest preimplantation stages of its growth, constitutes something less than a human individual. The embryo, they claim, is to be regarded as mere tissue, with no claim to individual identity or, *a fortiori*, to legal protection. This is merely an extension of the reasoning behind the proabortion movement. If a third-trimester fetus can be aborted with no ethical or legal consequences, then it seems only reasonable to conclude that embryos can be created and destroyed with impunity. A growing consensus sees such a conclusion as self-evident because of the potential usefulness of embryonic stem cells for creating medical therapies for a wide variety of neurological and other diseases. Even if embryos can be considered to be incipient human life, people ask, isn't it reasonable—and ethical—to use their stem cells in order to relieve the suffering of countless patients of Parkinson's or Alzheimer's disease, even if harvesting those cells inevitably destroys—kills— the embryo?

The answer to that question should be clear, although it goes very much against the reigning mentality in today's culture. In Romans 3.8, the apostle Paul lays down the basic ethical principle that governs the Church's approach to the matter: we may not do evil so that good may come. A good result does not justify an immoral action. If Orthodox ethicists have consistently condemned the use of embryonic stem cells and similar manipulations of life at its earliest stages, it is because they hold to the theory of immediate animation, the theory that human life begins at conception, which traditionally has been understood to be coterminous with fertilization. Once the nuclei of sperm and ovum unite, a genetically unique being exists. Under normal circumstances, that being will grow in a continuum from fertilization through birth and on to physical death. Orthodox tradition also holds that human life is created in the image of God and bears that image throughout its existence, before death and beyond the grave. It is that image that confers on the human individual the quality of "person" from the earliest stages of human development.

From the viewpoint of the Church, therefore, to destroy embryonic life is to destroy a human person. Even if we consider the potential good to be derived from embryonic stem cells, insofar as the harvesting of those cells destroys the embryo, it involves the killing of a newly created personal being. Since that act itself is inherently evil, there is no ultimate good to be derived from it. No moral calculus that weighs the good against the bad in this case has any validity, because before God, we may not do evil in order to obtain a good result.

This kind of thinking, once again, appears retrograde and repugnant to most people. They have been persuaded that ESCR holds an immense therapeutic potential, and they wonder at the Church's intransigent refusal to bless and support it. To many Orthodox Christians, on the other hand, the conflict here reflects as clearly as any other the fact that we are actually living in two different worlds, one governed by utilitarian expediency and the other by the gospel of Christ. We speak different moral languages because we fail to share the same moral perspectives and commitments. With radically different moral presuppositions, traditional Christianity and postmodern secular ethics remain worlds apart with regard to any resolution of moral conflicts. Although each one may be able to understand the other's position, we share no common basis, no "canonical content-full moral vision" that makes it possible for us to resolve in the public square bioethical or other moral disagreements.[3]

To paraphrase Dostoevsky once again, without God in this secular, pluralistic environment, anything is permissible, particularly if it can serve utilitarian ends such as improving human health and extending the life span. With God, on the other hand, and in obedience to God, we accept the moral requirement to refuse even the good when that purported good is purchased at the cost of destroying human life. From the perspective of the gospel, we may not save or ameliorate the conditions of one life by sacrificing another, except where that entails self-sacrifice (Jn 15.13). This is

---

[3]The expression in quotes belongs to Tristram Engelhardt. For a highly perceptive analysis of the problem of differing moral languages and intuitions that separate traditional (i.e., Orthodox) Christianity from ethical perspectives with a different values content, see his work: Tristram Engelhardt, *The Foundations of Christian Bioethics* (Lisse, Netherlands: Swets and Zeitlinger, 2000), esp. chap. 1. As he points out, "Moral acquaintances can be moral strangers" (37).

the work of Christ, accomplished once and for all by his death on the cross. As for ourselves, it is essential that we hold to the truth that human life finds its ultimate value and purpose beyond the limits of biological existence. Good health and a long life are desirable and worthy goals. They are so, however, only to the extent that they exist to further our growth toward what Orthodox tradition calls *theōsis*, or deification—eternal participation of the human person in divine life, the life of the Holy Trinity.

Our rejection of certain medical procedures that lead to the destruction of embryonic life, then, is grounded in our vision of the true purpose of human existence: not to improve or extend our life as an end in itself but to surrender that life, together with its suffering and its limitations, into the open arms of God.

In what follows, I would like to spell out the basic reasons for the Orthodox consensus regarding the manipulation of human embryos and efforts to clone human persons. This will entail, first of all, taking up the question of the beginning of human life. Then we will draw some conclusions regarding morally acceptable forms of stem cell research and the development of various therapies that make up what is called today "the new medicine."

When Does Human Life Begin?

Unlike their Roman Catholic counterparts, Orthodox theologians are reluctant to speak of a specific point at which God endows the newly created embryo with a soul. Western thought is marked by a certain dualism in this regard, holding that the soul is co-created with the body, or that the soul is infused into the body at some point after fertilization. To the Orthodox, this reifies or objectifies the soul, distinguishing it from the body as a separate entity. From the holistic perspective of the Greek Fathers, it would be more appropriate to speak of the body not as having or possessing a soul but as *being ensouled*. It is animated by the God-given *psychē*, or life principle, at every stage of its existence. Neither body nor soul ultimately exists without the other, even if physical death involves a certain separation of the soul from the flesh. The body (*sōma*) embraces flesh, soul, and spirit, and although the flesh "returns to dust," the bodily or somatic character of our existence abides into eternity.[4] This is why, adopting biblical imagery, we affirm that Christ's victory over death results not in the immortality of the soul but in the resurrection of the body.[5]

Therefore, rather than affirm that the human person receives and possesses a soul, as an entity distinct from the body, it would be more accurate to say that the person is an ensouled being, and is such from fertilization onward. The soul, in other words, is to be understood as the animating principle in human life that guides development of the person from fertilization through death and into the kingdom of heaven.

This way of thinking leads to the important conclusion that human life is sacred from its very beginning, since from its conception, it is an ensouled existence. As such, it is a personal

---

[4]See chap. 6 for a fuller discussion of the body. A valuable discussion of the relation between body, soul, and spirit in Greek patristic thought can be found in J.-Cl. Larchet, *Thérapeutique des maladies mentales* (Paris: Cerf, 1992), esp. chap. 1.

[5]See, in this regard, the thought-provoking article by John Garvey, "Ashes to Ashes: Toward a Christian Understanding of Death," *Commonweal* 141, no. 2 (January 30, 2004): 16–19.

existence, created in the image of God and endowed with a sanctity that destines it for eternal life.

The most pressing issue we have to face with regard to the use of embryonic stem cells and to cloning is the familiar, long-debated question, When does human life begin? Several years ago, I attempted to address this question by referring to recent discoveries in the field of embryology.[6] The conclusion I drew was that human life begins at conception—meaning fertilization, or syngamy—with the fusion of the nuclei of sperm and ovum to produce a single-cell **zygote**. It seemed to me that the continuum between fertilization and birth is such that no other point can reasonably be argued as marking life's actual beginning. While I still hold that view, it would be worthwhile to nuance the conclusions I drew, and to raise again the question as to whether those conclusions are based on sound scientific evidence. Let me proceed with a brief overview of the issue.

Throughout history, a number of answers have been given to the question of when human life begins. The basic choice is between "immediate" and "delayed" animation, or hominization; that is, whether the zygote itself can be considered to be a human individual (and not merely an amorphous bit of human tissue), or whether individuality actually begins at a later point, during or after the gestation period. Those who defend the latter view of delayed animation suggest a variety of possibilities. Some hold that human life, properly speaking, begins only with implantation of the fertilized ovum in the uterine wall; others hold that it begins only slightly later with the appearance of the neural streak, or

6John Breck, *The Sacred Gift of Life*, chap. 3.

primitive body axis, that signals the earliest development of the spinal cord and central nervous system. Others—often, it must be pointed out, with an agenda to preserve abortion rights—locate the first stage of truly human life at quickening, when the mother first feels the child move in her womb, or at birth, when the child takes its first gulp of air and begins to breathe on its own. Still others would withhold from a newborn child any claim to legal recognition and protection until the child proves to be free of serious genetic anomalies, impaired intelligence, and other defects. In this view, human life begins only when society says it does and confers the status of human being or person on the newborn infant.

There is no question in anyone's mind that from the point of fertilization, the newly created embryo is characterized by genetic uniqueness, or more precisely, genetic individuality. That unique genetic makeup does not of itself constitute the embryo, of course, but it will characterize each cell of the developing being throughout its lifetime. The twenty-three chromosomes received from each parent align themselves in a unique combination that produces new chains of DNA (deoxyribonucleic acid), which is both the blueprint and the fundamental building material of life. In early 1953, Francis Crick and James Watson of Cambridge University, with the collaboration of Rosalind Franklin and other scientists, produced a model of the DNA molecule that has enabled subsequent researchers to confirm its key role in human development, specifically in storing and transmitting hereditary information.[7] The molecule is structured as a double helix, rather like two

---

[7] For fairly nontechnical introductions to DNA science and the history of DNA research, see James D. Watson, *The Double Helix* (New York:

nested corkscrews. It consists of a "backbone" of two spiraling chains, linked by purine and pyrimidine base pairs: adenine-thymine and guanine-cytosine. These pairs, held together by hydrogen bonds, "spell out," in the letters A-T and G-C, the basic code of life. In each living being, the inherited genetic code is unique. Although it can be replicated through monozygotal, or "identical," twinning prior to implantation of the embryo in the uterine membrane, with fertilization a unique being has come into existence whose genome (genetic blueprint) is different from that of either parent. There is, then, no disagreement among embryologists as to the point at which genetic individuality begins. It begins "at the beginning," with the creation of the zygote.

What is less clear, and the point at issue, is whether genetic individuality is accompanied by developmental individuality. By this latter expression we mean the stage at which embryonic cells begin to differentiate such that they become increasingly specified, leading to the development of particular tissues and organs. That differentiation is caused in large measure by gene expression: individual genes, working in combination, have the effect of switching themselves on and off, beginning during the very early stages of embryo development and continuing throughout the lifetime of the organism. The question is, Does cellular differentiation begin in a definitive way during the preimplantation stage? Or does it begin only after implantation, with the radical transformation known as **gastrulation**, or singularity, when the capacity for twinning is lost and organogenesis, the production of specific organs, begins?

Penguin, 1968); and especially his recent and more detailed work, *DNA: The Secret of Life* (New York: Knopf, 2003).

The question may not seem momentous. But in fact it is crucial for determining the Church's stance on procedures such as *in vitro* fertilization (IVF), ESCR, and cloning. This is for a very simple reason. If fertilization establishes both genetic and developmental individuality, then we must affirm that human life begins with the creation of the zygote. If, however, cellular differentiation actually begins only with implantation, then we need to affirm that an individual human life begins only at that point. In this latter case, the so-called "preembryo" (prior to implantation) could properly be considered to be what has been called the "substratum of human life," the necessary biological prerequisite that holds the potential to become human life. But it would not be an individual human being as such, and much less a person.

To the minds of many specialists in this area, a decisive argument for delayed animation is the phenomenon known as **totipotency**, the capacity to generate a complete organism from an individual cell. *Totipotent* is a term used to describe the **blastomeres**, the individual, loosely associated embryonic cells produced in the early stages of mitosis. During this preimplantation period, one or more blastomeres can split off from the main cell cluster. Since each cell contains the full genome, and since individuation or specification through gene expression either has not begun or is at a very early stage, each blastomere or group of blastomeres can develop into a complete human being. This is what produces identical twins. Each individual cell at this stage is totipotent in that it possesses the same potential as the zygote to produce a new human life. This quality of the preimplantation embryo leads many people to reject the idea that the zygote itself can be considered an actual human being, and to hold to the theory of delayed animation.

Those who support this view of delayed animation do so not only because of totipotency and the fact that there is a question as to the true onset of developmental individuality. They also find a powerful, intuitive argument in the phenomenon that carries the unfortunate label "wastage." This refers to the vast number—estimates vary from 35 to 75 percent—of fertilized ova (embryos) that are spontaneously expelled from the mother's body before implantation and before she is even aware that she is pregnant.[8] These "mini-miscarriages" are part of the natural, God-given process of procreation. In themselves, the demise of these embryos poses no particular moral problem. The mother is not responsible for their loss, and since she is unaware of its occurrence, she need feel neither guilt nor any sense of regret.

In trying to explain the phenomenon of wastage to parishioners and other laypeople who have been concerned about it, I have usually placed it in the framework of theodicy—the seemingly irresolvable conflict between the image of a good God who is omniscient and omnipotent, and the reality of evil. To many people's minds, it is incomprehensible, even impossible, that God could allow such wastage, if indeed it involves actual human life—if the preimplantation embryo is in reality a human individual, bearer of the divine image and consequently an ensouled being. This in itself is enough to convince many people, including

[8]Proponents of the theory of delayed animation often argue that prior to implantation of one or more embryos, the woman is not pregnant; the term, they hold, is inappropriate at this stage. Those who hold to immediate animation consider the mother to be pregnant from the point at which the zygote is formed and begins to grow. It is interesting that many women claim to know they were pregnant during the first week of the embryo's existence, well before implantation.

a great many Catholic and Orthodox Christians, that human life begins not with fertilization but with singularity, or gastrulation, when, following implantation, the embryonic cells reorganize themselves to produce the primary germ layers of ectoderm, mesoderm and endoderm, followed by the development of the primitive streak. Prior to this radical reorganization of cellular material, they hold, it is inappropriate or simply wrong to consider the embryo to be developmentally individuated human life, to hold that it constitutes a living human being.

Those who defend a view of delayed animation also point to the relationship between mother and child that is essential for human personhood (defined as "Being *in communion*"). Without that relationship, which requires implantation and development in the womb, they would argue that the embryo created *in vitro* is in fact a "preembryo." As a fertilized egg, it deserves respect because of its potentiality, but it is not a human person. This implies that there is a fundamental—in philosophical language, an ontological—difference between an embryo created *in utero* and one created in the laboratory, at least insofar as the latter is not transferred to a womb for purposes of procreation. It also suggests that embryos expelled as wastage, prior to implantation and establishment of the mother-child relationship, are not actual human beings but simply hold the potential to become such. The question is, Does the embryo constitute a human being *in itself* apart from any personal relationship it may have with the mother? Or is that relationship the basic and indispensable factor in transforming a group of cells into an incipient human child?

If the theory of delayed animation is correct, then we could have no serious moral objections to manipulating or even destroying human embryos through procedures such as IVF, ESCR, and cloning. We could harvest embryonic stem cells from the preimplantation **blastocyst**, even though that would destroy the embryo; we could freeze "extra embryos" produced in a petri dish for the purpose of IVF, or use them for experimentation; and we could clone those cells to produce various medical therapies—all without significant moral consequences. Moreover, we would no longer feel any reluctance to perform an early abortion on victims of rape or incest. This is because we would believe that the embryo at this stage has not yet acquired developmental individuality, and therefore it should be regarded as merely the necessary precondition to actual human life, or to the life of an actual human being.

Despite the basically inexplicable phenomenon of wastage, I have argued for immediate animation in the belief that scientific evidence confirms that cellular differentiation actually begins with the onset of mitosis, shortly after fertilization.[9] Without going into the details, we can briefly note the following points that support this view.

The late French embryologist Jérôme Lejeune, with others in his field, has argued that the phenomenon of DNA **methylation** signals the onset of cellular differentiation from the two- to four-cell stage of mitosis (cleavage or segmentation).[10] A methyl (CH_3) addition to the cytosine base of the DNA serves as a marker to

[9]See Breck, *Sacred Gift of Life*, esp. 135–38, which provides relevant references.

[10]For a summary in English, see Jérôme Lejeune, *The Concentration Can* (San Francisco: Ignatius, 1992), esp. 34–48. Methylation should be understood as a process that involves "demethylation" and *de novo* or remethylation. Reprogramming of genomic methylation patterns occurs in the germ cells and

indicate gene expression from this early stage. That expression contributes toward differentiation in the individual cells. In other words, from this early point, the blastomeres are individually programmed, in limited fashion, to perform specific functions; they are programmed by what Lejeune calls the "primal formula" of embryonic development. If this is true (it has been established in mice and other animals; it remains to be confirmed in humans), it supports the view that developmental individuality character-izes the embryo from the earliest stages of its existence, well before implantation. It also means that the concept of totipotency is misleading. In fact, only the zygote is truly totipotent; the blas-tomeres are more appropriately described as pluripotent (capable of differentiating into one of many cell types), despite the fact that each one can potentially grow into a human individual.[11]

in preimplantation embryos, and contributes to the establishment of cellular totipotency. In certain animal species (mice, cows), the paternal genome undergoes rapid, active demethylation just after fertilization, whereas a sim-ilar phenomenon occurs more slowly and passively in the maternal genome. Remethylation occurs shortly before the time of implantation. Both genomes independently direct the process of segmentation, or cell division, up to the blastocyst stage (four or five days after fertilization and well before implan-tation) and are responsible for directing gene expression. See W. M. Rideout, K. Eggan, and R. Jaenisch, "Nuclear Cloning and Epigenetic Reprogramming of the Genome," *Science* 293 (August 10, 2001): 1093–98; H. R. Fairburn, L. E. Young, and B. D. Hendrich, "Epigenetic Reprogramming: How Now, Cloned Cow?" *Current Biology* 12 (January 22, 2002): R68–70; and M. R. W. Mann and M. S. Bartolomei, "Epigenetic Reprogramming in the Mam-malian Embryo: Struggle of the Clones," *Genome Biology* 2002, 3(2): reviews 1003.1–1003.4. I am very grateful to Terry (Juliana) Orr-Weaver of MIT, for providing me with these and other valuable materials on the topic of embryo development and cloning.

[11]It is important to note in this regard that "identical" twins are hardly iden-tical, even genetically. During the preimplantation stage of growth, genes

If this methylation theory is accurate, it confirms the view that the so-called "preembryo" grows in an unbroken continuum, becoming progressively what we misleadingly term an embryo, then a fetus, then a child. Consequently, we would have to affirm that human life begins with fertilization. And if so, the preimplantation embryo should be legally and socially acknowledged to be in the fullest sense a human being and deserves to be cherished and protected accordingly.

This is a critical issue that we need very much to resolve. For to date, the Roman Catholic and Orthodox churches, together with numerous Protestant Christians, have vigorously, even passionately, opposed the harvesting of stem cells from human embryos precisely because of the conviction that it destroys incipient human life, that it kills a human being. For similar reasons, the Roman magisterium (the Congregation for the Doctrine of the Faith) strongly opposes new procreative technologies such as IVF, because again it involves the creation and destruction of embryos—for purposes of experimentation, and because not all embryos produced *in vitro* can be transferred to the mother's uterus without the risk of multiple implantations and consequent pressure for "fetal reduction," the selective abortion of one or more of the children growing within the mother.

With regard to ESCR and cloning specifically, most Catholic and Orthodox ethicists have concluded that they are morally

express themselves somewhat differently in each cell or cell cluster, and each newly implanted embryo receives new *epigenetic* information from the uterus. While such twins share an identical genome, the obvious differences between adult twins indicate that those differences have their origins in the period prior to implantation.

unacceptable. Their opposition is based on the theory of immediate animation, the conviction that the soul is created at fertilization.[12] If it can be shown conclusively that the preimplantation embryo is in fact merely a substratum of human existence, that the phenomena of totipotency and wastage mean that it cannot be considered to be a human individual, then we would be obliged to drop our opposition to ESCR and human cloning, at least for therapeutic purposes.

Because there is a great deal of confusion over these matters, we should spell out briefly the difference between normal embryonic procreation and cloning. Cloning is achieved asexually by somatic-cell nuclear transfer. In this procedure, a fully differentiated somatic-cell[13] nucleus from the animal to be cloned is inserted

---

[12]Not all Roman Catholic ethicists hold to the theory of immediate animation. Although recent Vatican documents (*Donum Vitae*, 1987; *Evangelium Vitae*, 1995) imply that ensoulment occurs with fertilization, the language is somewhat ambiguous ("personal presence," "unity as a body and spirit"). Historically, the Catholic Church has defended the notion that the soul is "infused" by God two or more weeks after conception. Today, many influential Catholic ethicists (Norman Ford, Thomas Shannon, Robert Cefalo, et al.) argue for locating the beginning of human life at implantation, largely on grounds of totipotency and wastage. The notion of the soul's infusion at a specific moment, at conception or later, is foreign to Orthodox anthropology because of its dualistic overtones. This is why it seems preferable to use biblical language and state that the embryo *is*, rather than has or receives, a soul (cf. Gen 2.7, by the Spirit of God man *became* a living being). The question is whether that becoming, in the form of a new and ensouled creation, occurs immediately with fertilization or as the result of a process that is only completed with implantation.

[13]All cells in the body are somatic cells, with the exception of the germ, or sex, cells, also called gametes. Modifications introduced into germ cells become part of the organism's genetic legacy and carry down to future generations. This is not the case with somatic cells.

into an enucleated ovum (an ovum from which the nucleus has been removed). The somatic nucleus is fused to the host ovum by a small electric charge or in culture, and this initiates cleavage, or cell division. After four to six days, a blastocyst of some sixty-four cells forms, from which it is possible to harvest stem cells. In reproductive cloning, the stem cells would not be harvested; instead, the newly created embryo would be transferred to the womb of a surrogate mother and, if possible, brought to term. Cloning, therefore, creates no new or unique genome.

In summary, somatic-cell nuclear transfer is asexual. Nearly all of the genetic material is derived from the original somatic nucleus and hence the newly formed embryo has essentially the same genome as that of the original animal. And the cells that produce the embryo are already differentiated. Natural embryonic reproduction (traditional procreation), on the other hand, is sexual, involving the union of a male gamete with a female gamete. This produces a zygote whose genome is indeed unique, although it can be replicated through twinning and cloning. That zygote is an undifferentiated cell; differentiation will begin only after early embryonic development.

These differences between cloning and natural reproduction are significant. It has not yet proved possible to clone a human being and produce a viable human embryo by somatic-cell nuclear transfer, although attempts to do so are continuing in several countries, particularly in South Korea, Italy, and the United States.[14] These attempts, although they hold out the promise of

[14]The Raelian announcements of successful human reproduction through cloning were a hoax. Advanced Cell Technology, a Boston-based research company under the direction of its founder, Michael West, succeeded several

extraordinary new therapies, have made clear certain limitations inherent in the process of nuclear transfer. The presence of abnormal DNA methylation patterns in cloned embryos, for example, seems to be responsible for the low percentage of success in attempts to create clones of mice and bovines. Similar abnormal patterns seem to be present in cloned human cells. If so, the contentious argument over human cloning may in fact be moot.[15]

The fear that human cloning will indeed become a reality, however, has led to interesting, if troubling, questions. Will a human clone be an ensouled being?[16] More to the point for our purposes is the conclusion dawn by many people that a nonimplanted human or nonhuman embryo produced by somatic-cell nuclear transfer is not, for the reasons just given, a true embryo, even though it can potentially develop into a complete being (mouse, sheep, goat, cat, etc.). Since that embryo is the product of asexual

years ago in growing a cloned embryo to the six-cell stage. Recently, a research team in South Korea announced successful nuclear transfer in a procedure that could open the way to cloned human beings. On the other hand, the cloning of individual human cells for research purposes has long been routine.

[15]Fairburn et al., "Epigenetic Reprogramming," concludes with the following warning: "The discovery of aberrant DNA methylation patterns in cloned bovine embryos may be an important first step towards increasing the efficiency of [cloning]. But the differences in early methylation patterns between mice and cows provide strong evidence that what holds true for one mammal is not necessarily the case for all, and is a further reason why attempting to clone a human is simply out of the question."

[16]I have argued that human clones, if ever they become reality, will certainly be ensouled, personal beings. See John Breck, *God with Us: Critical Issues in Christian Life and Faith* (Crestwood, NY: St Vladimir's Seminary Press, 2003), 47–55.

reproductive techniques and possesses no unique genome, the question arises as to its moral status. Even if we reject the idea of harvesting stem cells from embryos created by fertilization, may we consider it morally acceptable to extract those cells from cloned human embryos?

Cloning of human cells and tissues has been practiced for years.[17] Most people can accept it without moral ambivalence, convinced that the scientific teams are working with human material but not with individuated human life, a conclusion that seems self-evident. Ambiguity remains, however, regarding the cloned embryo; is it human material, on the order of somatic cells (hair, skin, bone, blood, etc.), or is the embryonic clone itself to be accorded the status of a human individual? If it is merely human material, then the harvesting of its stem cells and the production of stem cell lines in the interests of creating new medical therapies would pose no ethical problems. (It is important to note that to those who defend a theory of delayed animation, there is no moral difference between such a procedure and the harvesting of stem cells from blastocysts created by sexual reproduction. Both are acceptable because neither involves an actual human individual.)

---

[17]Human stem cells have been cloned to facilitate skin grafts, bone marrow transplants, etc., as well as for pharmaceutical research. Kenneth Alonso, *Shall We Clone a Man? Genetic Engineering and the Issues of Life* (Atlanta: Allegro, 1999), makes an important point in this regard: "These [cloned] cells (as well as those more differentiated somatic cells from a diseased organ surgically removed, for example, or the cells of skin and intestine replaced daily), though possessing potentially the information necessary to replicate a whole human, are determinate and have identity. But they are not a life in the same sense as is the whole human. Clearly, then, there is more involved than biology in the determination of the human person" (68f).

As I have pointed out elsewhere,[18] by defending the position of immediate animation, we set up a major obstacle to research which could lead to the development of medicines and other therapies that can potentially cure a broad array of neurological and other diseases. Even though adult stem cells, as we shall see, hold extraordinary therapeutic potential, embryonic stem cells (including those produced by cloning) are easier and cheaper to harvest. Does God call us to oppose this potentially lifesaving and life-enhancing research? Or is our opposition simply a replay of the Church's response to the Copernican revolution and its condemnation of Galileo, a well-meaning but misinformed and misguided reaction against what science has discovered about the way God governs the universe?

Some people might argue that we cannot allow science to dictate the convictions of the Church. This well-intentioned objection is based on a misunderstanding of the relation between science and our faith. God is the ultimate source of all genuine knowledge, including knowledge gained through scientific inquiry. We should not lapse into a fundamentalist rejection of scientific findings simply because they call into question some aspects of our worldview. After all, we no longer find it necessary to argue for a flat earth or for "water above the firmament," since our cosmology now corresponds more closely to reality than did that of the author of Genesis.

With regard to the beginning of human life, then, we are faced today with momentous questions whose answers will determine

---

[18]"The Larger Question," a column in the Life in Christ series of the Orthodox Church in America web page, www.oca.org, August 2003.

how we respect, protect, and preserve human existence in the future. One of the most important of those questions concerns the nature and status of the preimplantation embryo. This can be finally answered only by determining exactly what occurs in the first two weeks of human life.

Until scientists can provide us with satisfactory answers to this fundamental question, we will be lacking critical information needed to make certain moral judgments about the nature and status of the embryo and, we might add, about human life altogether. For ultimately there is another basic question. Do we have the moral right—is it the will of God—to use ourselves to heal ourselves? Are we in some bizarre sense cannibalizing ourselves in the selfish interests of better health and longer life? Or is it God's will that we exploit—fully, yet respectfully and with great caution—the new knowledge and the new technologies at our disposal? Are we being called to beware of the increasingly slippery slope that has already produced a culture of death? Or does our capacity to use our own cells for therapeutic ends in fact enable us, for the first time and in nearly miraculous ways, to obey the command, "Physician, heal thyself"?

Manipulated Embryos and Designer Genes

The therapeutic usefulness of embryonic stem cells (ESCs) was first discovered in 1998 by James Thompson and his team at the University of Wisconsin. ESCs are undifferentiated cells with two important characteristics: they can be multiplied to create a permanent reservoir, and they can be induced to become differentiated cells that perform a specific function. Accordingly, the potential exists for stem cells to produce replacement tissue for the body (e.g., blood, nerve, muscle, brain) and even to create entire organs. Their therapeutic potential, therefore, is huge and awesome.

The extraordinary plasticity characteristic of ESCs has already led to the production of nerve, heart, muscle, and other cells used to treat laboratory animals. Until recently, it was thought that ESCs could produce only somatic cells. In May of 2003, however, the journal *Science* reported that a team of French and American researchers had transformed ESCs taken from mice into germ line cells, specifically into ova. These then produced an embryo by parthenogenesis (without the benefit of fertilization by sperm). The embryo remained viable for only a few days and was incapable of becoming implanted. The team leader, Guy Fuhrmann of the French *Centre National de Recherche Scientifique*, noted that they are presently testing to see if ESCs can produce male gametes as well. If they can, it means that stem cells retrieved from embryos have the potential to reproduce not only specific tissues and organs but also entire organisms, each with its unique genome.

The media has touted these successes so as to give the impression that a panacea for illness and aging lies just around the corner. It has given far less coverage to the dangers inherent in stem cell therapies, including their rejection by the autoimmune system and their occasional growth into lethal tumors. At this point (spring 2005), it is still too early to know whether ESCs will prove more useful in the development of various therapies than, for example, fetal tissue has been. In the early 1990s, scientists focused enthusiastically on fetal cells in their search for cures for diseases such as Parkinson's, ALS, and other neurological disorders. To date, results have been rather disappointing, although recent tests indicate that fetal cells may prove useful in the treatment of Huntington's chorea to relieve symptoms of spasticity and dementia.

The dangers and limitations of ESCs and fetal tissue need to be acknowledged. In themselves, though, they do not warrant a moratorium on research and experimentation. If a moratorium is indeed called for, it is on other grounds, namely, the moral status of the embryos and fetuses used and destroyed for these purposes. It is this concern that recently led the Russian Orthodox Church, under the leadership of Patriarch Alexis II, to threaten to excommunicate not only scientists who clone embryos in order to harvest their stem cells but even patients who seek to benefit from those cells. Although to some people this sounds extreme, grounds for this warning are found in the basic Christian principle that we may not sacrifice one life in the interest of saving another. To quote Richard Barnes, director of the New York State Catholic Conference, "We sympathize with those who suffer illness or disabilities that can potentially be aided by stem cell research. But nothing can justify the creation and killing of human beings for the purpose of possibly curing other human beings." This statement, of course, reflects the current official position of the Catholic Church, which holds to the theory of immediate animation. With most Orthodox Christians, the Roman Congregation for the Doctrine of the Faith believes that science and theology concur in viewing the preimplantation embryo as an actual, and not merely a potential, human being.

This perspective has also led many in both traditions to reject the distinction usually made between therapeutic and reproductive cloning. To those who defend the theory of immediate animation, any such distinction is nonexistent. If indeed the preimplantation embryo is a human being, and not just the substratum of human life, then creation of that embryo is *ipso facto* reproductive. If its stem cells are harvested, then the embryo dies and a human being is killed in the process.

A theory of delayed animation, however, leaves room for a legitimate distinction to be made between therapeutic and reproductive cloning. The latter would occur only with the transfer of the early embryo to the mother's womb. If such a transfer is rejected on principle, then researchers would be free to create embryos for the purpose of acquiring and manipulating their stem cells, without moral consequences. This is the conviction that lies behind the *Human Cloning Ban and Stem Cell Research Protection Act of 2003*, cosponsored by Senator Arlen Specter (R-PA), one of the most ardent supporters in Congress of ESC research. The act would allow for the cloning and manipulation of embryos for therapeutic purposes during the first fourteen days of their existence, after which, by law, those embryos would have to be destroyed. While this latter provision is to prevent reproductive cloning, including the creation of designer babies, to those who consider those embryos to be human beings, it marks another government-sponsored step toward the desecration of human life.[19] Everything, then, turns on the question, When does human life begin?

The matter of embryonic stem cell research cannot really be separated from another issue that is causing a tremendous stir

---

[19]The Specter bill prompted Senator Rick Santorum to propose a ban on cloning by introducing the *Human Cloning Prohibition Act of 2003*.

because of its potential long-term consequences. This is the issue of "designer genes," the modification of one's genome by introducing into it genetic material that has been altered for a specific purpose, either to replace defective genes in hopes of curing disease, or to enhance certain traits deemed desirable, such as height, strength, intelligence, and amiability.[20] One of the most vocal opponents of the "new eugenics" program that scientists are presently embarked on is Bill McKibben. In his recent book, *Enough: Staying Human in an Engineered Age*,[21] McKibben declares that "lured by the prospect of making better babies, we stand on the threshold of changing forever what it means to be human." As an example, he quotes Michael West, CEO of Advanced Cell Technology (ACT), who declared that "the dream of biologists is to have the sequence of DNA, the programming code of life, and to be able to edit it the way you can [edit] a document on a word processor."

Michael West has been vilified by everyone from the president to the pope because his company produced the first known human clone (although, as we noted, it survived only to the six-cell stage). To many minds, the ACT team proceeded with inadequate precautions and with blatant disregard for the legislative debate that might well have made its research illegal. It seemed that they plunged ahead with no consideration for the intrinsic value of human life.

---

[20]Gene therapy in somatic cells has been practiced successfully for many years. The question at issue concerns inserting genes into human embryos.

[21]Bill McKibben, *Enough: Staying Human in an Engineered Age* (New York: Times Books, 2003).

In the summer of 2003, I spoke at length with Michael West and came away from the conversation moderately relieved. He argued, in fact, that my position and his were "only a few days apart," since he believes that individuated human life—a living human being—comes into existence only with implantation and the appearance of the primitive streak. I did not point out the fact that if my position of immediate animation is correct, then those few days are equivalent to light years. But I did leave the conversation persuaded that he, like most other scientists working in the field, holds human life in the highest regard. These people are not the wanton desecrators they are so often depicted to be.

This said, however, the kind of caveat formulated by McKibben and others needs to be heard. The slippery slope is real, and pressures toward a new eugenics movement are powerful, perhaps irresistible. The human genome now has been sequenced, and the capacity does exist to "program the code of life." Although, with some radical exceptions, world opinion is solidly against human cloning for reproductive purposes, much less opposition has been voiced regarding the modification of the human germ line for purposes of "ameliorating" the human gene pool or "improving" inherited characteristics.[22] But as McKibben points out, those who engage in eugenics are captive to the "myth of the perfect child." Such perfection, or even the desire to accord our children

[22]See the following articles in *Hastings Center Report*: Nancy M. P. King, "Accident and Desire," *Hastings Center Report* (March–April 2003), 23–30; Mark Frankel, "Inheritable Genetic Modification and a Brave New World," *Hastings Center Report* (March–April 2003), 31–36. These articles discuss inadvertent germ line effects produced by gene transfer. Not all modifications introduced into the genome by these new technologies are intentional, nor do all of them represent improvements.

certain genetic advantages, will always remain unattainable. This is because of the laws of competition. Wealthy parents will seek to give their children an edge relative to the children's peers and so will program certain capabilities into the embryo. When a sibling comes along a few years later, however, technology will have advanced. This second child, then, will be further programmed with the latest genetic improvements. That child will inevitably outstrip its older sibling in as many ways as the new programming will allow. This means that there will be constant social and economic pressure to "upgrade" our children, much like the pressure to buy the latest version of computer software. The result will be to turn our children into products rather than autonomous persons. And utilitarianism will have achieved its final triumph.

Add to all of this the effects of natural curiosity ("Can it be done? If so, then do it!") and we have a formula for unbridled abuse. Perhaps the most appalling example to date is the one announced on July 3, 2003, concerning Norman Gleicher and his private New York–Chicago fertility group, Centers for Human Reproduction.[23] The group's research team created a human "shemale" by transplanting cells from a developing male embryo into a three-day-old female embryo. The resulting hybrid was androgynous, a hermaphrodite combining thoroughly programmed male and female characteristics. Supposedly undertaken to facilitate research toward various therapies, the experiment was roundly condemned by European scientists, one of whom declared, "This research happened in America, but I can't imagine it being accepted anywhere in Europe, I'm happy to say!" The obvious rejoinder is, "Just you wait . . ."

[23]www.ananova.com/news/story/sm_796295.html?menu.

Slightly less ominous, but a source of equal concern, is the grow-ing production of chimeras, life forms that are part human and part something else. Already in May of 1998, the journal *Science* reported that ACT scientists had created a transgenic cow, a human-bovine hybrid. Jose Cibelli and his team inserted the nucleus of a human somatic cell into the ovum of a cow, also in the interests of research. At the turn of the millennium, a San Francisco company announced it had created a strain of mice, a quarter of whose brain cells were human. And just recently, sci-entists at the Second Medical University in Shanghai, China, reported that they had fused "human skin cells with rabbit eggs [ova] to produce early stage embryos, which in turn are killed for their stem cells."[24] The research team justified the experiment by claiming it was a means for providing ESCs without sacrificing human embryos. Pro-life groups have raised their voices against the procedure, however, because of the mixing of human with animal cells. The chimeras of ancient Greek mythology, it seems, are prescient images of today's unsettling reality.

Ethical and Not-So-Ethical Alternatives

Where does all of this leave us? Are we destined to land in a heap at the bottom of the slippery slope, unable any longer to recog-nize ourselves as truly human or to appreciate ourselves as endowed with the image of God?

Fortunately, with regard to stem cells and their potential thera-peutic value, there are alternatives to ESCs that may well prove equally useful and effective. Perfecting those alternatives will not

[24]www.lifenews.com/bio53.html.

stop morally challenged researchers from creating chimeras and carelessly destroying embryos. But it might eliminate the need to use and abuse embryos as we do now, for purposes of developing successful and lucrative therapies to treat and possibly cure devastating diseases.

Of the alternatives now available or being developed that have been proposed as ways to eliminate the need to create embryos for their stem cells, we can mention and comment briefly on five: (1) "extra embryos" from IVF procedures, (2) parthenogenesis, (3) "master genes," (4) tissue engineering, and (5) adult stem cells.

(1) *Extra Embryos.* A growing number of voices, including those of pro-life activists, are urging governments to sanction the use of the hundreds of thousands of "extra embryos" that are left over from IVF procedures throughout the world.[25] These have been cryopreserved (frozen) either to be implanted in the mother's womb if the first series does not "take," or else to be used for experimentation, in order to perfect IVF techniques or to extract their stem cells. In rare cases, they have been put up for adoption and offered to sterile couples or to single women who wish to bear them and bring them to term. Normally, such frozen embryos are destroyed after about five years. Certainly it is far better and more reasonable, it is argued, that they be used to further reproductive technologies than that they be destroyed, allowed to die, or otherwise go to waste.

Orthodox and Roman Catholic ethicists tend to reject that logic on the grounds that those extra embryos should never have been

---

[25]It is estimated that there are some 400,000 such embryos in the United States alone.

created in the first place. The Catholic magisterium in fact condemns IVF altogether, as it does other forms of medically assisted procreation, because of what it perceives to be the immoral manipulation of human gametes and the embryos formed from them.[26] The Orthodox have been less outspoken about assisted reproduction in general. They have reached the clear consensus, however, that extra embryos should never be created and, *a fortiori*, that they should never be subjected to experimentation. The basis for this rejection once again is the principle enunciated in Romans 3.8, that we may not do evil so that good may come. However promising embryo research may be, however great the potential for therapies derived from embryonic stem cells, the ends simply do not justify the means.

(2) *Parthenogenesis.* Some people concerned with these issues have argued that a morally acceptable alternative to the harvesting of ESCs can be provided by the technique known as parthenogenesis. The term means literally "virgin birth" or "virginal generation." It consists in asexual reproduction without fertilization, in which an ovum is chemically induced to begin cell division. In February 2002, ACT scientists reported in the journal *Science* that they had created a line of stem cells by parthenogenesis; the ovum of a macaque monkey was chemically induced to begin segmentation.

The pressing ethical question is whether embryos created by parthenogenesis have the same moral status as those created by natural fertilization. The journal *Stem Cells* reported in early

[26]See especially the Congregation for the Doctrine of the Faith, "Instruction on Respect for Human Life in Its Origins and on the Dignity of Procreation" (*Donum Vitae*), February 22, 1987.

2003 that both mouse and human embryos had been produced by parthenogenesis. Since these could not gestate, some scientists concluded that they are unique and do not qualify as true embryos.

The reason such embryos cannot gestate, however, is because they lack a trophoblast (the outer layer of the blastocyst), which is essential for the formation of the placenta. They cannot grow because they cannot implant. Yet in all other respects, they are identical to ordinary embryos. If embryos derived parthenogenically from human cells are to be considered nonhuman simply because they cannot gestate, then any miscarried child would also have to be classified as nonhuman.

Others have argued that parthenogenically produced embryos are in a class apart because they are not the product of syngamy, the union of a male and a female gamete. Since they possess no unique genome, they are not endowed with genetic individuality and therefore are not human embryos in any conventional sense. Yet the same could hardly be said of an identical twin, whose genome is not unique either.

From the viewpoint of Christian anthropology, parthenogenic embryos possess the same moral status as any other human embryo. This does not mean, however, that the Church can sanction or bless the manipulation that produces them. If we speak of procreation rather than reproduction, it is because we understand that "God made them male and female," with the aim that they participate in God's ongoing work of creation (hence *procreation*). The divinely willed and divinely given means for continuing this creative activity is through the sexual union of a man and a woman. They become one flesh in relation to one another, a new creation that brings forth a further new creation in the form of the offspring who are born of their union. Parthenogenesis involves a manipulation and exploitation of gametes and the resulting embryos that reduces them to nothing more than reproductive material. Thereby it thwarts their God-given purpose and deprives them of human dignity. As an alternative method for providing stem cells for therapeutic purposes, the parthenogenic creation of embryos, then, is morally unacceptable.

(3) *Master Genes.* In May of 2003, the scientific journal *Cell* reported the discovery of so-called master genes. These are the genes that are responsible for the pluripotency of embryonic stem cells. Scientists named them "nanog genes," from the mythical Celtic land of Tir Nan Og, whose inhabitants remain forever young. By inserting copies of human nanog or master genes into embryonic mouse cells, researchers found they could prevent those cells from differentiating. They successfully inhibited gene expression so that the cells functioned as pluripotent stem cells. This seemed to be an acceptable alternative to the harvesting of ESCs, because no human embryos were created.

Nevertheless, in perfecting the technique, a great many human embryos have to be destroyed. Moreover, the entire process involves creating chimeras using human cells. Although the hope is to reprogram human adult cells by activating their master genes, and thus to restore them to a state of pluripotency so they can function as stem cells, those who defend a theory of immediate animation find that the procedure raises irresolvable problems that lead inevitably to the abuse of human embryos.

(4) *Tissue Engineering.* A far more positive development is one that promises to eliminate both the need for organ transplants and the use of ESCs. This is the new field of tissue engineering, which aims to create in the laboratory cells, body tissues, and even vital organs. For many years, scientists have been able to culture cells to produce two-dimensional tissues. The problem has been to create three-dimensional structures that will allow for the making of entire organs. In early 2003, scientists at Clemson University and the Medical University of South Carolina announced through the local media that they had developed a process for tissue printing that could produce just such 3-D models. They did so by creating a scaffold using alternating layers of cellular clumps and a supergel. The device adapted for this purpose is a simple desktop printer, modified so that living cells and the gel fill the printer cartridges, and the nozzle prints alternating layers onto a glass slide. As the cells grow and form clusters, the gel is washed away. This gradually produces cellular structures that can develop into whole organs. The potential of this procedure is such that it has been backed by the National Institutes of Health. The research team estimates, however, that they are still five to ten years away from true organ construction.

The promise of this new technology, even in its infancy, is indeed extraordinary. If it can be perfected, it would eliminate organ harvesting and transplants, just as it would put an end to the creation and destruction of human embryos in order to acquire their stem cells. Tissue engineering also requires stem cells. Those cells, however, need not come from embryos. They can be harvested from an inexhaustible reservoir of adult somatic cells, and it is there that we need to direct our attention.

(5) *Adult Stem Cells.* Whether we opt for a theory of immediate or delayed animation, there is only one real solution to the problem of the use and abuse of human embryos. This is to limit our quest for stem cells to those found in sources such as placentas, umbilical cords, and adult somatic cells. In late 2001, Catherine Verfaillie of the University of Minnesota announced her discovery of MAPCs—multipotent adult progenitor cells. Commonly referred to as adult stem cells, these have roughly the same therapeutic potential as ESCs.[27] The fact that they have been found in such diverse sources as blood, bone marrow, skin, fat, brain tissue, and even baby teeth suggests that practically any cell in the human body might have its DNA rendered pluripotent so that the cytoplasm can be reprogrammed to initiate the gene expression needed for the production of specific tissues. Any adult somatic cell, in other words, might contain the potential to serve in the place of embryonic stem cells.[28]

---

[27] Through 2002, adult stem cells were considered by most scientists to be multipotent rather than pluripotent, as are ESCs. It was believed that they were programmed only for specific tissues (hematopoietic stem cells, for example, thought to be able to produce only blood-cell lines), and that they could not be multiplied indefinitely to produce undifferentiated cells. More recent research indicates that such limitations may not exist, as suggested by our continuing discussion and the following footnote.

[28] Ted Peters of the Center for Theology and the Natural Sciences suggests this possibility in his article "Embryonic Persons in the Cloning and Stem Cell Debates," *Theology and Science* 1, no. 1 (2003): 51–77. He writes, "On the list of scientific questions is this one: how does the cytoplasm program the DNA nucleus so as to express the genes that make specific tissue? Once this is learned and technical control of gene expression is attained, then perhaps the cytoplasm in virtually any somatic cell could be reprogrammed for specific gene expression" (66).

To date, no safe and effective treatment using ESCs has been developed for use with human beings. Reports have recently been published, nevertheless, indicating that human embryonic cells can repair myelin, the insulating layer that surrounds nerve fibers. Rats, paralyzed because of spinal cord injuries, have been successfully treated, and the hope is that the technique might prove adaptable to impaired patients. For the time being, however, it remains merely a hope.

Adult stem cells (ASCs), on the other hand, have already proven to be highly effective in clinical trials using both animal and human subjects. Areas in which successes have been recorded include immune deficiency disorders, stroke, sickle-cell anemia, leukemia (as well as lymphoma, pancreatic cancer, and other cancers), heart disease, type 1 diabetes, spinal cord injuries, and Parkinson's disease. The following list was culled from various sources, including scientific journals and Internet sites.[29]

* April 2002: California Parkinson's patient Dennis Turner was treated with his own neural stem cells. His symptoms were reduced by over 80 percent.

* February 2003: Sixteen-year-old Dimitri Bonneville's heart was pierced by a three-inch nail. ASCs from his own blood were injected into his coronary artery, providing significant improvement.

---

[29]For useful information, check the following: http://stemcells.nih.gov; http://excr.nih.gov; www.prolifeinfo.org; www.americancatholic.org; www.ananova.com/news/science&discovery; *New England Journal of Medicine*; *Journal of the American Medical Association*; *Hastings Center Report*; *National Catholic Bioethics Quarterly* (esp. vol. 1, no. 2, Summer 2001).

* March 2003: The *Journal of Clinical Investigation* reported successful treatment of diabetes using ASCs. Bone-marrow stem cells were converted into insulin-producing beta cells to replace damaged pancreas cells.

* April 2003: The British journal *Nature* reported that brain stem cells injected into mice relieved symptoms of muscular sclerosis. They stimulated myelin-producing cells to repair lesions on the nerve sheaths.

Throughout 2003 and 2004, research continued, proving the usefulness of adult stem cells for various therapies and their availability in a broad variety of body tissues.[30] Most recently, in December 2004, German researchers reported that cells extracted from the fat of a seven-year-old girl helped repair her damaged skull; fat cells, in other words, can apparently generate bone in human beings. At the same time, scientists at the Johns Hopkins School of Medicine and elsewhere announced the discovery of a reservoir of stem cells in the heart. These, together with stem cells derived from bone marrow, offer new hope for repairing damaged heart tissue.

These successes with adult stem cells have been matched, if not surpassed, by stem cells taken from placentas and umbilical cords. Cord blood cells, for example, recently provided a cure for

[30]See, for example, the following articles from the journal *Gene Therapy*: K. K. Hirschi and M. A. Godell, "Hematopoietic, Vascular and Cardiac Fates of Bone-Marrow-Derived Stem Cells," *Gene Therapy* 9, no. 10 (May 2002): 648–52; and A. Peister et al., "Stable Transfection of MSCs by Electroporation," *Gene Therapy* 11, no. 2 (January 2004): 224–28. ("Human marrow stromal cells [hMSCs] are an attractive source of adult stem cells for autologous cell and gene therapy" [from the abstract].)

three-year-old Spencer Barsh, who was afflicted with adrenoleukodystrophy (ALD), an inherited metabolic disorder in which the myelin sheath of nerve fibers in the brain is progressively lost. Leukemia and diabetes afflicting fifty-four-year-old Steven Sprague were cured by a cord blood transplant. In fact, successes with cord blood have been hardly less than spectacular, offering further evidence that stem cells from sources other than embryos are readily available and possess a remarkable therapeutic potential.[31]

It should be noted, nevertheless, that adult stem cells, like their embryonic counterparts, pose certain risks and exhibit clear limitations. They are relatively rare in the human body (although, as we have seen, they exist in a wide variety of tissues and organs) and are difficult to isolate in the pure form that makes them therapeutically useful. If the donor of such cells suffers from a genetic disorder, transplanting his or her stem cells might transfer that disorder to the recipient. And there remains the possibility of rejection by the recipient's autoimmune system. These and other factors lead many scientists, whose moral integrity is unquestionable, to conclude that successful development of regenerative medicine requires and justifies continued research on embryonic stem cells.[32]

---

[31]The National Cord Blood Program of the New York Blood Center has collected over twenty thousand donations of cord blood, which can be banked for future use. See the report of the NCBP, dated June 12, 2003, www.nybloodcenter.org.

[32]On this issue, see the study produced by the National Research Council, *Stem Cells and the Future of Regenerative Medicine* (Washington, D.C.: National Academy Press, 2002), esp. 19–39 on adult and embryonic stem cells and their promise and limitations.

Conclusions

Orthodox Christians, including priests and theologians, often hold that Scripture and liturgical tradition support the notion of immediate rather than delayed animation. They point to Old Testament passages such as Psalm 138/139.13, where the psalmist declares that God "knit" him together in his mother's womb, or Jeremiah 1.5, where God assures the prophet, "Before I formed you in the womb I knew you, and before you were born I consecrated you." One of the most frequently cited New Testament passages is Luke 1.39–42, which recounts Mary's visit to her kinswoman Elizabeth. When Elizabeth heard Mary's greeting, "the babe leaped in her womb" in acknowledgment that Mary was herself pregnant with the Messiah.

None of these passages, however, is decisive. Nor is the fact that the Church celebrates feasts of the conceptions of Christ, the Virgin Mary, and John the Baptist. Each of these scriptural and liturgical texts affirms the idea that individual, even personal, life exists "in the womb." Yet by "womb" (*beten, koilia*: stomach, belly, body cavity) the biblical passages signify the uterus, since the ancient Hebrews knew nothing of ovulation and fallopian tubes. The biblical and liturgical witness, in other words, can easily be understood to support a notion of delayed animation that situates the beginning of human life at implantation.

If many of us feel uncomfortable with this conclusion, it is largely because of the famous slippery slope. We are well aware that multitudes of embryos have been created and destroyed for utilitarian purposes. If we are to slow the slide toward unrestricted manipulation of human life at its elemental stage, then we feel we must insist against wind and tide that life begins at fertilization. That insistence, however, as we have tried to show, is well grounded, based on evidence provided by specialists in the field of embryology as well as on the Church's ages-old intuition. If we are correct, there is no such thing as a preembryo, an intermediate stage between gametes and embryonic life. Accordingly, despite the objections to the theory of immediate animation raised by the totipotency of the blastomeres and the phenomenon of wastage, we continue to defend the notion that conception occurs at a protracted moment when the nuclei of sperm and ovum unite to create the genetically unique, single-cell zygote.

To remain faithful to the perspective of Orthodox anthropology, then, we must resist any reformulation of the notion of conception that would define it as an ongoing process, one that might last as long as ten or twelve days, beginning with formation of the zygote and coming to completion only following implantation and the appearance of the neural streak. As much as the scientific community, pharmaceuticals industry, and other vested interests might want to convince us of some theory of delayed animation, we must continue to insist, on the basis of sound scientific evidence, that individuated human life begins during the very first stages of mitosis.

Manipulation of the human embryo is one of the most difficult ethical issues we have to grapple with today. Yet it is also one of the most important, since the approach we take depends on our understanding of the meaning and value of human life itself. In this postmodern world, there are enormous pressures to treat life as a commodity to be exploited for utilitarian ends. It is our responsibility, as members of the body of Christ, to perceive and proclaim a different truth: that human life derives from and is destined to return to the transcendent life of the Holy Trinity.

Human life—from fertilization until biological death—is a sacred gift, destined for a greater and more glorious existence than our minds and hearts can imagine. Our moral responsibility, before God and before each other, is to acknowledge that sacredness by preserving and protecting human life at each and every stage of its existence. It is to behold the presence and purpose of God in the developing embryo as well as in the dying patient, and to minister to both with unfailing love and compassion. Thereby we can honor the divine image in all human persons, from conception to death, as we surrender them into the merciful hands of the author of life.

Glossary

blastomere. A cell of the early embryo, produced as the fertilized ovum divides before it implants in the wall of the uterus. A blastomere is a totipotent cell produced by mitosis, the segmentation or division of the original one-cell **zygote**. (The **totipotency** of the early embryonic cells is lost once the embryo implants in the uterine membrane.) Each blastomere contains the full genome and thus contains the potential to develop into a unique organism.

blastula, blastocyst. A spherical cluster of cells, formed four or five days after fertilization. From about the sixty-four-cell stage, the **morula** (an aggregation of **blastomeres**) becomes a blastocyst, a hollow, fluid-filled sphere, concave and bounded by a single layer of cells. The cavity, or blastocoele, forms the inner portion of the blastocyst and contains embryonic stem cells. The outer cell layer becomes the trophoblast (or chorion), which produces the placenta; the inner cell mass becomes the embryoblast. This organizes itself to form the embryonic disc. During the fourth week, this develops into a tube-shaped **gastrula.**

DNA (deoxyribonucleic acid). The "genetic blueprint" of life; a molecule, found mainly in the nuclei of cells, which determines inherited characteristics. The molecular basis of heredity, DNA is constructed of a double helix held together by hydrogen bonds, plus oxygen and carbon. The helical chains are linked by the purine and pyrimidine bases ATGC: adenine, thymine, guanine, cytosine. These bases code hereditary information in the polynucleotide chain of DNA. (Uracil replaces thymine as one of the bases that codes genetic information in the polynucleotide chain of RNA.) The human genome is composed of some 35,000 genes, segments of DNA that code for proteins.

epigenesis. The development of a plant or animal from an egg or spore through a series of processes in which unorganized cell masses differentiate into organs and organ systems. Epigenesis is the process that leads from the genotype (the genetic composition of an organism) to the phenotype (the physical properties or makeup of the organism that results from the interaction of the genotype and the environment).

fertilization. The process by which a male gamete (sex cell) and a female gamete unite to form a genetically unique single-cell

zygote and thereby initiate the growth of a new individual. Fertilization initiates this development by restoring in the zygote the full somatic number of forty-six chromosomes, arranged in twenty-three pairs, half received from the ovum and half from the sperm.

gastrulation. The process, occurring with implantation, by which the cells of the embryo become specialized to form various body tissues and organs. Gastrulation marks the stage of embryonic development that leads to singularity (loss of the capacity for twinning) and the onset of organogenesis (development of organs). Gastrulation establishes the three primary germ layers of the embryo: the ectoderm (forms brain, nerve, skin, hair, nail, and eye tissues), the mesoderm (forms heart, bones, muscles, glands, circulatory system, and reproductive organs), and the endoderm (forms the epithelium of the digestive tract and respiratory system, and produces certain internal organs).

methyl, methylation. A chemical marker that indicates the beginning of gene expression, as different genes are activated in the early embryo. Methyl is a chemical substance (CH_3) derived from methane by the removal of one hydrogen atom. (Methane [CH_4], a gaseous hydrocarbon, is produced by the decomposition of organic matter.) Methylation refers to the introduction of a methyl group, as into the cytosine base of DNA. (See chap. 3, note 9.)

morula. A globular mass of **blastomeres**, beginning at about the sixteen-cell stage of embryonic development. The morula is produced by the cleavage or segmentation of the **zygote** through mitosis. (*Morula*: from the Latin and Greek for "mulberry.")

totipotency. The capacity of an individual **blastomere** to develop into a genetically unique organism, or to differentiate (become transformed into any of that organism's cells or tissues). Pluripotent or multipotent cells (such as stem cells) can develop into specific cells or tissues but not into complete organisms. Totipotency is lost at **gastrulation.**

zygote. The single-cell organism created by the union of a male gamete (sex cell) and a female gamete, containing a full complement of forty-six chromosomes. The zygote marks the first stage in an individual's growth and is both genetically and developmentally unique.

chapter four

THE SACREDNESS
OF NEWBORN LIFE

Jesus took a child and put him in the midst of them. And taking him in his arms, he said to them, "Whoever receives such a child in my name receives me; and whoever receives me, receives not me but him who sent me."
— Mark 9.36–37

Recent discussions in bioethics have focused the public's attention almost exclusively on the issues of embryonic stem cell research and the cloning of human embryos. These are crucial issues that threaten to undermine the conviction, basic to Orthodox Christianity, that human life is inherently sacred and deserves to be nurtured and protected from conception until death.[1]

Ethicists who share this belief in the sacredness of human life are caught up in cultural warfare with opposing forces whose chief motivations are the potential profits to be made from stem

[1]This chapter appeared in a slightly modified form in John Breck, "The Sacredness of Newborn Life," *St Vladimir's Theological Quarterly* 47, no. 2 (2003): 221–27.

cell based therapies, together with preservation of the right to abortion on demand at any stage of a pregnancy. For if the government were to acknowledge that human life begins at conception—meaning fertilization—then it would jeopardize the future of embryo experimentation and undermine the principle of unrestricted abortion enshrined in judicial interpretations of *Roe v. Wade.*

The dust cloud kicked up by this struggle has obscured a related matter that is equally significant in today's utilitarian atmosphere, which places rights over responsibilities and convenience over the value of persons. This is the issue of the newborn child and our social, familial, and ecclesial responsibilities in that child's regard. In what follows, I would like to move away from the question of the child *in vitro* or *in utero* and turn our attention to the way God calls us to welcome the newborn infant, particularly when that child is marked by some form of genetic anomaly or physical disability.

As we advance into this new millennium, it is clear that our children are facing a crisis worse than they have ever known. Children have always been threatened by poverty, forced labor, prostitution, and abandonment. Today, we have to add to that list such threats as partial-birth abortion, which kills a child as it emerges from the womb; infanticide, recommended by ethicists who believe a child must demonstrate a viability free of genetic defects in order to have the right to live; together with an appalling increase in violence, both in school and at home. Recent estimates suggest that one American child in five lives in poverty and that one in six suffers from hunger. Although drug use is down relative to its levels of ten years ago, it is concentrated today in certain sectors of society—and not only the poorest—and, as the French writer Francois Chateaubriand said about love, it "devastates the souls in which it reigns."

In 1999, the whole world came to know the name of Littleton, Colorado. This obscure western town became a symbol of the violence and wanton killing committed increasingly by youngsters against their own kind. Hospital emergency rooms are visited by a growing number of children who have been physically and sexually abused. Much of that abuse has been perpetrated by Christian parents and clergy. In Europe as well as in the United States, certain forms of violence directed against the very young have become virtually institutionalized. We may note, for example, gross neglect and abuse in the foster care system; or the incarceration of teenagers with adults in our state prisons, where the frequency of rape makes their punishment, by any civilized standard, "cruel and unusual." And it is clear that the responsibility for these kinds of violence lies in large part with social and economic systems that favor the wealthy and the powerful over the poor and the defenseless.

In the face of all of this, we can well understand why so many of our young people no longer find any meaning to life or hope for their future. In many parts of the world, children are born to become either victims or aggressors, or both. (Think, for example, of the generations of Lebanese and Palestinian youths who have spent their entire childhoods in a world at war—and the children of Iraq who are swiftly joining their ranks.)

To be sure, this is a one-sided and pessimistic view of the situation that gives too little consideration to the many children who are nourished by loving families and supported by intelligent and effective social structures. Nevertheless, there is no denying that a great many children today find themselves in a crisis not of their own making. It is incumbent on us, therefore, as members of the body of Christ, to seek out ways to ameliorate this critical situation faced by our children even before the time of their birth. This is all the more necessary when it is a matter of those children marked with disabilities, who by that very fact are systematically marginalized and often threatened with extinction.

The Newborn Child and the Newborn Christ

Who in fact is this one we know and welcome as the newborn child?

To answer the question, Christian anthropology refers us to Christology. To understand who we are, we need to begin with the image of the eternal Son of God, who is the archetype of our humanity, who became flesh by assuming the fullness of our human condition and our human destiny, including death. A mystery envelops every child, a mystery whose key lies in the image of the Christ child. This is true whether the child in question is born thriving or born dead, whether that child is welcomed with loving affection or aborted as an unwanted nuisance.

"When the fullness of time came," St Paul tells us, "God sent forth his Son, born of a woman, born under the law" (Gal 4.4). This is the child prophesied by Isaiah: "Behold, a virgin will conceive and bear a child, and shall call his name Emmanuel," which means "God is with us" (Is 7.14). This child, born of a humble virgin, is described by the author of the Epistle to the Hebrews in remarkably exalted language: "In these last days [God] has spoken to us by a Son, whom he appointed the heir of all things, through whom also he created the world. This Son reflects the glory of God and bears the very stamp of his nature, upholding the universe by his word of power" (Heb 1.2–3). The apostle Paul adds to this extraordinary affirmation, "In him the whole fullness of deity dwells bodily, and you have come to fullness of life in him, who is the head of all rule and authority" (Col 2.9–10). Every human existence finds its fulfillment in the person of the one whom the kontakion of the Nativity proclaims to be "this little child, the eternal God."

The true meaning of Christ's incarnation is revealed to us in the liturgy and in the iconography of the Church. It is there that we find graphically portrayed the "descent" of him who contains in himself the fullness, the *plērōma*, of divinity. By that descent—that kenotic or self-abasing movement toward our fallen state (Phil 2.7)—this divine Son was able to assume our humanity and transfigure it into the glory that he possessed with the Father before the foundation of the world (cf. Jn 17.5).

Within the Orthodox tradition, two principal icons depict the incarnation of the Son of God in the person of the Christ child. The most well known is the icon of Christmas, the Lord's nativity. This is an image of the ideal family, comprising Mary, Joseph, and the infant Jesus. It is all the more ideal because it so eloquently represents both the poverty and the abandonment that weigh on them. These painful conditions presage the journey that the child himself will undertake, a journey which will lead him to the Cross and to death. Even at his birth, the child is wrapped not in swaddling clothes but in a shroud, and he is laid not in a manger but on an altar of sacrifice. His ostensible father, Joseph, is shown under attack by demonic doubt concerning the paternity of this newborn infant.[2] And Mary herself gazes into the infinite distance, contemplating the mystery of a birth that will lead ineluctably to suffering, both for the child and for his mother.

Nevertheless, as in the icons called *Hodigitria,* or "Guide," or still more in those that evoke the *Eleousa, Umileniye,* or "Tenderness,*" the principal theme of the icon of the Nativity is that of *gift.* What Mary has received as a gift from the Father she presents to the world in a supreme gesture of love. Through her prayer, but also by her physical being, welcoming the Christ child into her womb, the Mother of God offers herself and her child, so that in him and by him the world might be transformed from the corruption of death to the glory and beauty of eternal life.

This motif appears as well in those icons known as "the Sign." This is the second sacred image which represents—which renders present and accessible in the experience of the worshiper—the mystery of God incarnate. Here, Mary appears as the *Orante,* the Virgin Mother who makes ceaseless supplication on behalf of us all. Bearing the Christ child in her womb, she offers him for the life of the world. Her womb, as the liturgical texts declare, is more spacious than the heavens, since it contains the Incomprehensible

---

[2]This is one interpretation of the figure standing before Joseph in the corner of the icon. Other interpreters have seen here the representation of a shepherd, who comes to announce the glad tidings to the child's "ostensible father." Still others identify this figure with the prophet Isaiah, who declares to Joseph that the prophecy of Is 7.13 has been fulfilled: a virgin has given birth to a child, Emmanuel.

and Uncontainable One. This antinomy is repeatedly expressed by the liturgy of the Nativity feast. One of the major themes of that celebration holds that the incarnation of Christ occurred *atreptos*, "without change." This means that the Son of God became the son of Mary without surrendering his divinity, without changing his essential identity.

> Beholding him [Adam, who represents all of humanity] who was created in his image and likeness, fallen because of his transgression, Jesus bowed the heavens and came down. He dwelt within the womb of a Virgin without undergoing change, so that within her he would reform the deformed Adam, who cried out to him, "Glory to your appearance, my Redeemer and my God!"
>
> —Compline, Nativity Vigil

The aposticha verses of this same service declare, "The Word assumed flesh but did not separate himself from the Father." He was God, and he remains God for all eternity.

The liturgy of the Nativity feast gives eloquent expression to this ineffable gesture of total humility, by which the author of creation "humbled himself, becoming obedient unto death, even death upon a cross" (Phil 2.8). According to the Nicene Symbol of Faith, this kenōsis or self-abasement occurred "for us men and for our salvation."

> Beholding man, the work of his own hands, destined for perdition, the Creator bowed the heavens and came down. From the pure and holy Virgin he clothed himself

in the fullness of human existence and truly took flesh,
for he has covered himself with glory.
—Matins of Nativity, Ode 1

The salvation accomplished by the incarnate Son, however, is not limited to delivering us from perdition, to liberating mankind from bondage to death and corruption. If the eternal God became a little child in the womb of the Virgin, it was in order to lead us along the pathway known in Orthodox ascetic tradition as the way of "purification, illumination, and deification."

> O our defender Christ, you have covered with shame the enemy of mortal man, now that you have ineffably taken flesh as a shield and, in this form, you have given us the gift of deification. For it is the desire for that gift that caused us to fall from above into the pit of darkness.
> —Matins of Nativity, Ode 7

These sacred images and liturgical texts recall several themes that throw light on the mystery of the Incarnation. At the same time, they clarify another mystery: that of the newborn child. If the eternal Word is the archetype of the human person—if he is both the first and the last Adam—he is also, by virtue of his nativity in the flesh, the archetype of every child who is born into this world. As author of life, as creator and redeemer, he submits himself to the conditions to which every child is subjected.

> Today is born of the Virgin the One who holds all
> creation in his hands.
> As a mortal, he, the incomprehensible One, is wrapped
> in swaddling clothes.

As God, he is laid in a manger, he who in the beginning
established the heavens.
He takes as food his mother's milk, he who poured out
manna to his people in the wilderness.
He, the Bridegroom of the Church, invites the Magi.
He, the son of the Virgin, accepts their gifts.
We worship your Nativity, O Christ.
Grant us to behold your holy Theophany!
—Nativity, Troparion of the Ninth Hour

The divine child, born of a virgin, accepts to be wrapped in swaddling clothes and laid in a manger in order to liberate mankind, like Lazarus, from the shroud of the dead and to raise us up from the depths of death and corruption. He who fed the Israelites in the desert feeds himself from his mother's milk, in order that he might become Eucharist, the heavenly bread that feeds the multitudes. He who invites the magi accepts their gifts, in order to foreshadow the offering of his own life as the supreme gift, the supreme sacrifice that works out the world's salvation.

God accepts to humble himself through the incarnation for a single reason: because he loves the world he has created and longs to seek and find, to save and glorify the children who bear his divine image. His purpose is to restore Adam to his original purity and innocence. To do so, the Son of God assumes the humility and innocence proper only to little children. For children are the very image of the Innocent One, the spotless Lamb who represents the perfect offering to God the Father. According to St Gregory Palamas, "Before the mind becomes embroiled with them, the passions which are naturally implanted in children conduce not to sin but to the sustaining of nature. For this reason they are not at that stage evil."[3] The child is thus the icon of Christ, as Christ is the icon, the prototypical image, of the child. This includes not only the newborn but also all those who become like little children in order to enter the kingdom of heaven (Mt 18.3–5; 19.14; cf. Jn 1.12).

In the Church's iconography and liturgy, we thus find a great many themes that illustrate the intimate relationship between the incarnate Christ and the newborn child. There is the theme of the family, united by prayer and by love; the theme of the mother who receives from God the child she will offer back to him as a sacrifice of praise; and the theme of the Innocent One, whose vocation is to offer himself to others wholly and freely, with a love that knows no limit.

Who, in fact, is this newborn child we are called to welcome, protect, nurture, and love?

He or she is the image of Christ, the Son of God, who, "without change," became the son of Mary for the salvation of the world and the deification of all those who receive him with thanksgiving and devotion. "To all who received him," the evangelist John tells us, "to all those who believed in his name, he gave power to become children of God" (1.12). To become a child of God is to

---

[3]St Gregory Palamas, "To the Most Reverend Nun Xenia," 42, in *The Philokalia*, vol. 4, eds. G. E. H. Palmer, Philip Sherrard, and Kallistos Ware (London: Faber and Faber, 1995), 310.

return to our original state of innocence, purity, and beauty, but also of vulnerability, which characterized the first human person, fashioned in the image of his creator. This is the Adamic state, proper to every newborn child. Yet it is a state soon lost in a world of sin and violence, where the innocent, inside or outside the womb, are massacred like the little children of Bethlehem.

The newborn child bears within himself the divine image, the image of Christ, and with that image comes the possibility for deification. But this tiny infant also bears within himself the seeds of corruption. The continuous and arduous struggle between the two—between deification and corruption—will lead him inevitably along the pathway of suffering and death. The newborn child is an image of the Christ child, but he is also an image of Christ crucified.

Welcoming the Newborn Child

If the child born into this world is indeed an image or icon of Christ, he will also become the image of his parents. We live in an age in which the traditional role of the parents has largely been rejected as a relic of a distant past. For virtues such as religious faith, altruism, obedience, honor, rectitude, and civility we have substituted egotistical attitudes of autoidolatry, self-gratification, in-your-face aggressiveness, and cutthroat competition, tempered only by a concern to think and act in a way regarded by others as politically correct. And parents are expected to inculcate such distorted attitudes in their children. Pressures behind such expectations come from our social and cultural milieu, conditioned as it is by television, films, and other media. Quite naturally, our children, like their parents, are increasingly obsessed with the Internet, an extraordinary instrument of communication but one that transmits anything and everything in the name of information.

Rather than lose ourselves in a fruitless quest for some idealized pretechnological age of the past, though, we need to ask a question. Is it possible for us today to reconsider the role and the responsibilities of parents in a way that stresses spiritual values over self-centered attitudes? If not, then we are facing a greater crisis than most of us imagine. For the first responsibility of parents—in fact, their basic vocation—is to reflect to their children the image of God, an image of truth, faithfulness, integrity, and love.

The parents, however, do not bring up their children in isolation. Their role in raising their offspring is complemented by the activity of other members of the Church. At least four basic actions are indispensable for raising our young appropriately, actions that need to be undertaken and sustained both at home and in the parish community. Children need to be *welcomed, nourished, educated, and loved.*

The welcoming of a child is a complicated matter that requires a great deal of preparation. First of all, the parents need to prepare themselves to assume both the pregnancy itself and the material and moral obligations that become theirs following the birth. Preparation of this kind requires an ongoing attitude of prayer, by which the parents make a ceaseless offering to God both of their child and of themselves. Yet their prayer is necessarily the prayer of the Christian community as well.

The eighth day after the birth, the child receives a name, often of a saint commemorated on the day of the birth. This creates a vital link between the newborn infant and a member of the eternal communion of saints. The prayer offered by the priest at the laying on of hands asks God "that the light of your countenance might shine upon your servant (Name), and that the Cross of your only Son be impressed on his/her heart and thoughts." This is first of all a request for a blessing. Then it goes on to ask for protection against "the vanity of the world and every evil counsel of the enemy."

As soon as the name is given, the Church, by its liturgical prayer, associates the newborn child with Christ. This unites the child with Christ's crucifixion and also with his victory over demonic power and over death. This intimate link between the child and Christ will be reaffirmed when the child is baptized, chrismated, and then "churched," introduced into the communion of the faithful on the fortieth day after the birth. The final prayer offered for the mother on that day captures just this emphasis.

> O God the Father Almighty, who by your mighty-voiced Prophet Isaiah foretold to us the incarnation through a Virgin of your Only-begotten Son and our God; who in these latter days, by your good pleasure and the cooperation of the Holy Spirit, for our salvation, and because of thy boundless compassion, graciously willed to become a babe by her. . . . Do now, O Lord, who preserves children, bless this infant, together with his/her parents and his/her sponsors; and grant that, in due season, he/she may be united, through water and the Spirit of the new birth, to your holy flock of reason-endowed sheep, which is called by the name of your Christ.

The Church's welcome of the newborn child thus comprises not only baptism, recognized as the rite of initiation, but also the prior giving of a name, which signifies for the child that he or she is inscribed in the Book of Life (Phil 4.3; Rev 3.5; 21.27).

This ecclesial welcome is, of course, to be more than a mere formality. To ensure that it represents a genuine integration of the child into the family of God, which will provide appropriate nurturing and spiritual formation, the community appoints godparents—spiritual elders who assume primary responsibility for the religious and spiritual development of the child, all the while embracing that child with abundant love and affection. The godparents are called to work in close relationship with the parents and the parish community, to provide the child with needed spiritual nourishment and training. It is they as well who, during childhood trials or adolescent crises, offer loving support not only to the child but also to the child's parents.

It's deeply regrettable that we have lost any real sense of the importance of godparents in the lives and formation of our children. The Church in its wisdom grants to these sponsors roles and responsibilities that the parents are incapable of assuming because of their lack of objectivity. The newborn child needs to be welcomed, nourished, educated, and loved not only by its own parents but also by the Church family, represented above all by the godmother and godfather. (This is why at least one, if not both, must be a faithful and active member of an Orthodox parish.) It is incumbent on us to recover the true meaning of sponsorship within the Church and to support by every means possible the service rendered by godparents within our parish communities. Our children today are in very great need of their ministry, and it is our obligation before God to respond appropriately and decisively to that need.

Children with Disabilities

Everything we have said to this point makes it clear that the child who comes into the world possesses an absolute and inviolable personal value. The similarity between his image and Christ's derives from the fact that from conception, that child bears the image of his creator. From his birth, and by the very fact of his existence, he bears a visible witness to the beauty, the innocence, and the humility of our Savior. Child of God and child of Adam, he is endowed with the sacred gift of life, whose ultimate purpose is to enable him to share fully and intimately in the very life of God.

But can we affirm the same thing with regard to handicapped children, those born with deformities or disabilities? If the newborn child is marked by genetic defects, if his face lacks any semblance of beauty or her brain is damaged, does that child possess the same honor and have a right to the same protection as a "normal" child who is in good physical condition? If the question seems offensive, we need nonetheless to raise it today. This is because more and more self-proclaimed guardians of public morality argue that each newborn infant should give proof of her viability and her "human value" before society grants her the right to live.

That sort of attitude represents an extreme form of utilitarianism, one based on sheer expediency. Utilitarianism is gaining ground today in Western Europe as well as in the United States. Its deconstructionist approach to ethical analysis rejects every absolute norm—every standard, principle, or truth—and locates the criteria for all moral decision-making within the immediate situation itself. The result is moral relativism, with a consequent breakdown in respect for God and other persons. Where moral absolutes are systematically rejected, the inevitable effects of sin are to substitute expediency for principle and self-interest for sacrificial love.

From this utilitarian perspective, the human person is defined by strictly functional criteria: consciousness, for example, with the rational and motor capacities necessary to make decisions and take action. These are criteria of social utility, derived from a philosophical position that places function above being. The simple fact that one exists is no longer sufficient for that individual to qualify as a person, worthy of respect and legal protection. That individual must be able to think and act rationally and be endowed with the capacity to contribute actively and positively to social life. Otherwise, the argument goes, society has no obligation whatsoever to assume the financial and psychological burdens that a profoundly handicapped person imposes on it.

Those who preach this kind of utilitarianism propose a gamut of disabilities that render the child marginalized, a prime candidate for abortion or infanticide. Others who tend to be more conservative or traditional will often accept a first trimester abortion yet reject unconditionally the killing of a newborn child. On the other hand, they recognize the appropriateness of refusing sustained treatment to children born with terminal illnesses or severe disabilities such as anencephaly, Tay-Sachs disease, or the Lesch-Nyhan syndrome. Each of these results from genetic anomalies that bring on premature death, often within hours of birth. In such cases, as we may all agree, medical treatment should be strictly palliative, caring for the child's comfort and allowing the parents to hold their dying infant. No heroic efforts should be undertaken which merely extend biological existence artificially, since in cases like these, such efforts merely prolong the dying process. (This, by the way, is a rule of thumb that should apply to any terminally ill patient, one whose prognosis indicates clearly that he or she is suffering the irreversible consequences of an accident or disease and has lost all capacity for self-sustained existence.)[4]

Many of today's utilitarians, however, are much more radical. They include in the category of the "nonviable" (those who have no claim to being persons in the true sense) even Down's syndrome children (those afflicted with trisomy 21, an extra twenty-first chromosome.) In Joseph Fletcher's view, for example, a Down's child is not a person because of the profound intellectual deficiency that usually accompanies the anomaly. Such children, pejoratively referred to as mongoloid, are accordingly to be eliminated by abortion or by infanticide.[5]

There are two comments I would like to make. First of all, the sacred character of human life, which God himself invests in the child at its conception, does not in any way depend on the physical or mental health of the individual, nor is it a function of the quality of one's DNA. The dignity of "person" is bestowed by God, not by human convention. This is why an embryo, like a

[4]We return to this theme in the final chapter.

[5]J. Fletcher, "The 'Right' to Live and the 'Right' to Die," *Humanist* 34 (July–August 1974): 12–15; see also Richard C. Sparks, *To Treat or Not to Treat: Bioethics and the Handicapped Newborn* (New York: Paulist, 1988), chap. 4, esp. 250ff.

STAGES ON LIFE'S WAY

patient in deep coma, is and remains a person in the fullest sense of the term. And this is why infanticide can never be sanctioned or blessed by the Church. Whereas palliative care and gestures of love offered to a profoundly handicapped infant are always morally obligatory, the expediency of infanticide, including partial-birth abortion, must be rejected as an act of murder.

The second comment I'd like to make is more personal. Anyone who has known or lived with Down's syndrome persons knows the difficulties and challenges of raising and educating them. Their physical and emotional needs can be extreme and exhausting. But those who care for them also know how much such a child—and they always remain a child—gives joy and love to the family and all those around them.[6]

I often think back to the late 1960s and early '70s, when my wife and I had frequent contact with Marie (Masha, to her friends), the Down's syndrome child of a former professor at the St Sergius Theological Institute in Paris. Every Holy Friday, Masha, dressed all in black, lived the agony of the crucified Christ, and every Pascha morning, she rejoiced at his resurrection. Her face was radiant and her joy palpable. The entire parish community, which had embraced her unconditionally, was profoundly enriched by her presence and her prayer.

One day we were invited by Masha's mother to share a meal with her family. As my wife and I entered the child's room—at that time

---

[6]It is not only Down's children who so bless a family that receives them with love. See Flannery O'Connor's remarkable "Introduction to 'A Memoir of Mary Ann,'" in S. and R. Fitzgerald, *Mystery and Manners* (New York: Noonday, 1962, 1969), 213–28.

she must have been about forty years old—we found her busy playing. All the while she was talking to a photograph of her godfather, a beloved and long-deceased priest who had also been a dear friend of ours. Masha spoke with him, just as little children speak casually with angels. There was nothing artificial about it, nothing at all contrived. She was carrying on a conversation with her godfather, that's all. And he was most definitely present, in some indefinable but unmistakable way, a way that was absolutely real. Masha spoke to him now in French, now in Russian. When she noticed our presence, she greeted us with a smile—in English. We later learned from a family acquaintance that her mother had long before taught her to recite several prayers in German.

An exceptional child, yes. But Masha was exceptional because of the love and the tender compassion she received from her parents and others who cared for her, persons whose lives were profoundly touched and blessed by her presence, her faith, and her love.

Do we really want to live in a world devoid of persons like Masha, just because *in utero* genetic testing exists and abortions are legal? I desperately hope we don't. Yet the new eugenics that has gripped this country is rapidly moving us toward a "final solution" in which no genetic anomaly will be tolerated, no "defective" child will be born or allowed to live.

How, then, should we welcome a disabled child? Just as we would want to be welcomed ourselves, as we would want our own healthy children to be welcomed. Where genetic or other deformations are so deleterious that the child is destined to a brief existence marked by acute pain, where death stares the child in the face day by day and moment by moment, there we can certainly opt for strictly palliative care. There, once again, medical heroics have no place, no justification. Biological existence is not an end in itself, to be preserved at all costs despite intractable and dehumanizing suffering that no pain management can adequately relieve. Rather, charity demands that in such cases the medical team do all in its power to provide whatever comfort is possible and to prepare the child for a gentle and peaceful death.

Yet it is our responsibility, as members of the body of Christ, to accompany the child, together with the child's parents, along the difficult pathway that stretches before them, and by our ceaseless prayer on their behalf, to surrender them into the open hands of the God of love and of life.

Cherishing the Newborn Child

With regard to every newborn child, and disabled children in particular, we need to keep certain points in mind. First of all, every child born into the world is gifted by our creator with absolute value and personal worth. Consequently, to recall an oft repeated affirmation of Olivier Clément: every child without exception "is worthy of infinite compassion."[7]

From conception until death, the child is a person, a bearer of the divine image, whose primary vocation is to conform increasingly to the likeness of God. This vocation consists in a long and difficult quest to acquire virtues or divine energies, such as justice, wisdom, beauty, compassion, and love. Human life is sacred from its

[7]For a brief and highly sensitive treatment of this theme that reveals just such compassion, see John Chryssavgis, *The Body of Christ: A Place of Welcome for People with Disabilities* (Minneapolis: Light and Life, 2002).

origin because it is created in the image of God and called to assume the ascetic struggle that leads toward divine perfection. It is this exalted vocation that transforms every individual existence into personal life. This is sacred life, since it originates from an act of the Father's creative love, and its ultimate end is to glorify and share eternally in the personal, communal life of the Holy Trinity.

Second, we need to remember that every newborn infant is essentially a child of the Church. Each one is created and called to become an ecclesial being, an integral member of the body of Christ. Therefore, it is our responsibility as adult members of that body, to assure that the children of our families and our parish communities are welcomed, nurtured, educated, and loved with a devotion and faithfulness that reflect the unshakable faithfulness and crucified love that Christ offers to us.

Finally, with regard to disabled children, we need to remind ourselves constantly of one basic truth. The innocent victim *par excellence* is Jesus Christ himself. He, the eternal Son of God, made himself utterly vulnerable in order to accomplish the greatest gesture of love we can imagine. As the Suffering Servant, "He was despised and rejected by men; a man of sorrows, and acquainted with grief; and as one from whom men hide their faces he was despised, and we esteemed him not. . . . But he was wounded for our transgressions, he was bruised for our iniquities; upon him was the chastisement that made us whole, and with his stripes we are healed" (Is 53.3, 5).

It is precisely this image of the Suffering Servant, fulfilled in the person of Jesus, that affirms and confirms the infinite value of disabled children, and obliges us to welcome them with gratitude and with love. The handicapped person—together with those who care for that person with patience, courage, and selfless devotion—is the very image of the suffering Son of God. In that person, we have a continual confirmation of St Paul's paradoxical observation: the power of God is made perfect in weakness (2 Cor 12.9).

The so-called normal child born into this world can benefit from a broad spectrum of practically inexhaustible possibilities. This is not true of the disabled newborn, who will suffer all of his life the consequences of some severe malfunctioning of his body or mind. In order that his infirmity not reach to the depths of his soul, we need to assume the responsibility to welcome him with compassion, understanding, courage, and an abundance of affection. That is, to welcome him as Christ welcomes us, with our own spiritual defects, weaknesses, and suffering.[8]

Who, then, is this newborn child who comes into the world?

Whatever the state of his health, whatever his defects or disabilities, he is an icon of Christ and a gift from God, both for his family and for the Church. Consequently, we are invited to welcome

---

[8]It is perhaps necessary to add that in a family into which a disabled child is born, the parents need to be especially sensitive to that child's siblings. The disabled child will require more attention and more resources than the other children, and it is of the utmost importance that those siblings not feel neglected or less favored. Here again, godparents can play a crucial role in helping to maintain an atmosphere of harmony and mutual support within the household.

him with open arms and to do for him what we are always called to do for one another: to offer him as a sacrifice of praise and thanksgiving to the God who is the author of his life, just as he is of our own. "Thine own of thine own, we offer unto thee." We should make this liturgical, priestly gesture whenever a child is born. Receiving him from God as a unique and infinitely precious gift, we offer him back to God by our prayer, by our love, and by the compassionate and attentive care we give him.

At the same time, we assume fully and without hesitation the life of this infant, whatever his mental or physical condition. Both in the family and in the ecclesial community, we welcome this child as the magi and shepherds welcomed the child Jesus. And we commit ourselves to do all in our power in order that this child, like Jesus himself, might grow in wisdom and stature, and that the grace of God might repose on him.

chapter five
ON ADDICTIONS AND FAMILY SYSTEMS

Lyn Breck

It is God's wish that each day we should be renewed and start up again with a virtuous change of will, and with a renewal of mind.
—St Isaac the Syrian, *The Wisdom of St Isaac the Syrian*

All things are lawful for me, but not all things are helpful. All things are lawful for me, but I will not be enslaved by anything.
—1 Corinthians 6.12

Defining the Problem

It was two a.m. Rita stumbled down the stairs toward the kitchen. Shaking and anxious, she held onto the banister to steady herself, then felt the cold tile floor beneath her feet as she made her way down the hall. Not wanting to wake her husband, Stan, she cautiously opened the freezer door and searched for the turkey. Her tension eased when she felt the bottle of vodka inside the frozen bird. Bracing herself, she began to pull it out. It wouldn't budge. Removing the entire turkey from the freezer, she placed it on the table, then used her foot to steady it as she pulled at the bottle once more. The bird slipped, careened onto the floor, and glided across the kitchen, the bottle still firmly inside. Tense and sweating, Rita heaved the slippery mess back onto the table, then decided the sink would work better. She hoisted the carcass into the sink and once more began pulling, this time with more success. Suddenly Stan appeared at the kitchen door. "Rita," he blurted, "what are you doing?" He saw the bottle now clenched in her hand, with the bird still in the sink. "Oh my God, Rita, you're an alcoholic!"

Rita had been hiding her alcoholism for twenty years, or so she thought. Some people around her knew. Those closest to her, however, didn't want to believe it. They were unable, or unwilling, to piece together her history of absenteeism, the DUI charge, the fall down the stairs, her moodiness, her late night trips to the store. She was actually in late stage alcoholism and struggling with the invasive "detox" symptoms of shakes and sweats. Only another drink would stop the symptoms, and then only temporarily. After the turkey episode, her husband was in shock, and so were her children.

This story and others you'll find in this chapter are true, though names and some details have been changed to preserve anonymity. They are the stories of many families. Most, in fact, are misinformed about the disease of addiction and are unable to recognize it when it occurs in their midst. Addictions of different kinds are rampant throughout our country: in homes, schools, workplaces, churches, and organizations such as the military and the government. Without treatment, an addict's behavior doesn't change. This is because addiction provokes a modification in brain chemistry that requires therapy—both medical and spiritual—if a genuine healing process is to begin. Without such therapy, addicts manifest the symptoms of addiction even when they give up the addicting substances or behaviors.

In this chapter, we will consider the immense toll that addictions and other forms of dysfunction take in all areas of our lives. Virginia Satir, a well-known family therapist, used to say that 96 percent of all American families are dysfunctional, and the other 4 percent are lying. This is a humorous way of making the point that in our society, addictions and other forms of dysfunctional behavior, whether mild or acute, are nearly universal. My purpose here will be to look specifically at the most common addictions, including codependency, alcohol and drug dependency, sex addiction, workaholism, and religiosity. We want to consider the roles that trauma and loss often play in the development of addictions. Then too we will explore the effects of addictive behavior on other family members. This will require that we introduce the concept of "family systems theory" to provide a framework for understanding the interconnectedness of members of an addictive family.

By God's grace and with appropriate therapy, recovery from addictions is possible, and a portion of this chapter will be devoted to questions of intervention and treatment. Then we will consider a series of delicate topics: the way our parishes function as family systems, how the Church tends to respond to addictive behaviors, and what a recovery-oriented church might look like, particularly in an

Orthodox setting. A significant number of Orthodox parishes were founded by people who came from countries where cultural alcoholism abounds and dysfunctional or unhealthy behavioral symptoms of the disease are considered normal. We need to challenge these age-old notions and the codependent responses they elicit. We need as well to create educational programs, both for our parishes and for our seminaries, to help Orthodox faithful understand and deal appropriately with addiction in all its forms. It is our hope that the following information will make a small contribution in that direction. At the outset, attention will be devoted to addictive behaviors as a bioethical problem, to how addictive behaviors lead to spiritual bankruptcy, and to how spiritual growth can occur through the healing process.

Ethical Aspects of Addictions

Why does a book on Orthodox bioethics feature a chapter like this? Because addictions affect body, mind, and soul. Our calling as Christians is to reflect the divine image in which we were created. Addictions, however, erode that image and make it less and less compatible with the holy. Serious health problems, accompanied by significant physical symptoms, make it virtually impossible to obey St Paul's command to "glorify God in and through our bodies" (1 Cor 6). Human neurophysiological capacity is a God-given gift that requires appropriate care to function properly. Brain chemistry is affected by what we put into our bodies and the behaviors we choose. We need to be wise stewards of our lives, our bodies, our emotions, and our choices. All of these choices, in the final analysis, are related to the state of our soul. These are, in fact, ethical choices. In the addictive state, cognitive abilities are clouded as the addict becomes increasingly preoccupied with the addicting substance and marked by impaired judgment. Rather than seeking the mind of Christ, addicts tend to compromise their moral values and embrace a secret life of deception. As the person sinks ever deeper into addiction, their spirit becomes enslaved to a form of idolatry. Simply put, the addicting substances or behaviors become more important than God, family, work, and life itself.

The very essence of our Christian being is communal, but under circumstances of addiction, true community life becomes all but impossible. An undivided focus on the object of the addiction prevents the addict from becoming an integral member of the body of Christ. The addict instead devotes time and attention to acquiring the addicting substance or engaging in the addicting activity (such as gambling, sex, computer games, high-risk sports) or to ensuring an adequate supply of the stimulus and recovering from the effects of its use. The call to holiness is abandoned in a desperate search for a high.

On some level, addictions are a veiled and misguided manifestation of our natural longing for God, an attempt to fill a void that ultimately can be filled only by life in Christ, who is the true physician of our bodies and souls. Long ago, before the coming of Christ, Old Testament prophets witnessed to and proclaimed "divine ethics," a morality in keeping with the will of God. God proclaimed through Ezekiel, "I will give you a new heart and put a new spirit within you; I will remove your heart of stone . . . and give you a heart of flesh" (Ezek 36.26). This passage goes on to affirm that by the indwelling of God's Spirit, each person will live in conformity with God's ways.

During Holy Week, we sing, "Turn not away Thy face from Thy servant, for I am afflicted; hear me speedily, draw near unto my soul and deliver it!" At some point in the addictive process, that turning back to God (*metanoia*, repentance) becomes possible. Once this occurs, the addicted person becomes a coworker with God, advancing toward his or her healing. Then the person can reclaim the ethical values lost with the addiction, making amends and embracing a life of spiritual growth through the process of recovery.

In Orthodox Christian practice, the prayers in preparation for Holy Communion help to strengthen the longing for holiness: "O Savior, sanctify my mind, my soul, my heart and my body, and grant me, O Master, to approach the fearful Mysteries [communion]."[1] When the faithful approach the chalice to receive the bread and wine, each person is addressed by the priest: "The servant (or handmaid) of God (Name), receives the holy and precious Body and Blood of our Lord and God and Savior, Jesus Christ, for the remission of sins and unto life everlasting." These holy gifts they receive "for the healing of soul and body."

Addictions fall squarely within the realm of bioethical considerations because their consequences are life damaging, even life threatening. They jeopardize the spiritual and physical well being of individuals, families, and communities. Yet despite the fact that addictions have devastating consequences, they can also become a means of grace.

---

[1] *Prayer Book*, 4th ed. rev. (Jordanville, NY: Holy Trinity Monastery, 1986), 345.

Defining and Identifying Addictions

The term addiction refers to an unhealthy relationship with mind-altering substances or behaviors, which has life-damaging consequences. This definition, proposed by John Bradshaw[2] in many of his workshops, is applicable to all addictions, not just alcoholism. More generally, we can speak of addiction in terms of the model proposed by Alcoholics Anonymous (AA). Step 1 of AA and other Twelve Step programs acknowledges that a person is "powerless" over the particular addictive substance or behavior and that the person's life "has become unmanageable."

Addictions occur most often in those who become predisposed to the illness through a combination of their genetic makeup and their lifestyle choices. Just as those who have a family history of heart attacks need to lower their risk by exercising and eating a healthy diet, so those with a family history of addictions are also at risk and need to make lifestyle choices that will promote good health. This said, however, we need to stress that those without any such family history are not immune to developing addictions.

Over the past several decades, addictions have been recognized as diseases that are chronic, progressive, and if untreated, deadly. Typically they unfold in three stages: early, middle, and late. One of the basic characteristics of addiction is denial; addicts generally refuse to admit they are ill. When the level of denial reaches that of self-deception, they are usually not even aware that they have a problem. Denial is also characteristic of family members and others who live close to the addict. Denial is not lying. It is

[2]A counselor and theologian, John Bradshaw is associated with the Center for Creative Growth and is author of half a dozen bestselling books in the field of family and related therapy.

the ability to close out or transform the facts in order to minimize the pain of reality.

How do we know when behavior is addictive? Specific symptoms outlined in the section "Examples of Addictions" later in this chapter will suggest answers to this question. The main thing is to know what to look for, to trust our observations, and to notice the progressive severity of symptoms in both the addict and the family involved.

Finding an appropriate path toward recovery depends on correctly identifying the problem, and diagnosis is not always straightforward. People who struggle with compulsive or addictive behavior yet whose problems are minor will not necessarily fit the profile of an addict. On the other hand, not all persons who manifest serious dysfunctional behavior are addicts; for example, those afflicted with schizophrenia, ADD, or sociopathic disorders. One must ask if the problem in question is really addiction. Often a single meeting between a concerned friend or family member and an addictions specialist (consult the Yellow Pages) will answer the question.

Statistics

Millions of people in this country are directly affected by addictions and addictive behavior. All those who live, work, or attend school or church with addicted people are themselves affected.

In the United States, alcohol-related auto accidents claim some 20,000 lives each year.[3] Thirty-six percent of convicted offenders

---

[3]Bureau of Justice statistics, www.safetycops.com/drunk_driving.htm.

in correctional institutions were drinking at the time of the offense. In 2001, nearly 1.5 million drivers were arrested for driving under the influence (alcohol or narcotics). This amounts to one arrest for every 137 licensed drivers.

Six out of ten adult children of alcoholics become alcoholics themselves. When both parents are alcoholics, the probability that their offspring will become addicted rises to 80 percent. It is no secret that drugs and alcohol are rampant on our college campuses. Intoxication leads to a breakdown in values and morality because inhibitions are weakened. At one college, it was determined that 60 percent of students who engaged in sexual activity were under the influence at the time. The result is a dramatic increase over the last decades in sexually transmitted diseases, sexual assaults, and abortions.

It is estimated that 90 percent of sexual assaults occur when the perpetrator is high on drugs or alcohol. One out of every six boys will be sexually abused before the age of eighteen, as will one out of every four girls. Pedophilia, one facet of sexual addiction, is a widespread affliction that damages the lives of vast numbers of children. The latest national survey holds that there are 374,270 registered sex offenders in the United States alone.[4] The global effect of such addiction can be seen in the millions of women and children in Southeast Asia and Africa who are victims of sex trafficking. Recent reports note the high incidence of sexual abuse in the refugee camps set up throughout South Asia in the wake of the 2004 earthquake and tsunami.

[4]www.nationalalertregistry.com.

Eight out of every ten people in America gamble, although of course not everyone who gambles is addicted to the activity. Gambling behavior is played out in a wide variety of forms and environments, from the simple purchasing of a lottery ticket in a grocery store to high stakes casinos, sporting events, and Internet poker. Any of these can become compulsive and unmanageable. Most compulsive gamblers are male; only 3 percent of those in treatment are female. In one state, a study of compulsive gamblers revealed that the average amount of money a person owed when they first sought treatment was in the neighborhood of $45,000. About 75 percent of those included in this study admitted that at one point they had thought of suicide as a solution. Seventeen percent had actually attempted suicide. The rate of suicide attempts among gamblers is six times the national average and the highest among all those with mental illnesses. Compulsive gamblers create other societal problems as well. Seventy-eight percent have committed a gambling-related felony, 22 percent have cashed bad checks, and 18 percent have embezzled funds.[5]

There are no available statistics regarding work addiction, referred to popularly as "workaholism." Suffice it to say that workaholism is rampant throughout this society and has significant and harmful social ramifications.

Religious addiction and abuse in religious settings is also widespread. In every confession, including Orthodoxy, God becomes for some people, both clergy and laity, the drug of choice and the means for controlling other people.

[5]Mary Heineman, *Losing Your Shirt* (Center City, MN: Hazelden, 1992), xvi, xvii.

Situations like these indicate the broad range of addictions in our society, as well as how pervasive and damaging they are. Addictions and their effects span all the stages on life's way. They are responsible for untold numbers of unwanted pregnancies resulting from unprotected sex, as well as for the spread of sexually transmitted diseases. During gestation, the fetus is especially vulnerable to the mother's use of drugs and alcohol, leading to developmental difficulties such as fetal alcohol syndrome. Crack babies come into the world with life-threatening detox symptoms (diarrhea, intestinal cramping, chronic runny nose and eyes). The families thus involved attempt to put on a good face while they fall apart under the influence of the addict in their midst. Marriages break on the rocks of addiction, and children are among the chief victims. Throughout life's various stages, we encounter a seemingly limitless number of crises which may be provoked by addiction: disabilities resulting from addiction-related accidents, the deterioration of physical health, mental illness, incarceration, and finally premature, addiction-related death.

Family Systems

Family Systems Theory

An exploration of addictions generally necessitates looking into the ways in which addictive and other dysfunctional behaviors bear on the lives of the household. The effects of addictive behavior are never restricted to the person alone; we are all interconnected, and the ties that bind families and other close communities are particularly strong. If our goal is to be holy as God is holy, then we need to explore the ways that our behavior as persons as well as in family groups, including our parishes, either fosters or detracts from this goal. Family systems theory can facilitate this task.

Family systems theory developed out of the field of psychiatry in the 1950s through the initial work of Murray Bowen. Other well-known clinicians, such as Virginia Satir, Jay Haley, and Salvador Menuchin, have shed a great deal of light on family dynamics, while offering effective strategies for healing, particularly in situations of addiction.

In the family systems approach, the development of trust within families is paramount, as is the facilitation of patterns of communication that enhance this trust. An intergenerational perspective on the family sheds light on the way issues and emotional legacies are transmitted from parent to child. Some of the most common intergenerational patterns that descend the family tree are rigid, black-and-white thinking (all or nothing, zero or ten); a heightened need for approval; a tendency to blame others and transfer shame and chronic anxiety; and the burden of feeling compulsively responsible for the happiness of others. These represent the very antithesis of the kind of life the gospel calls us to lead.

At first glance, family systems theory may seem to be a purely secular science. To the contrary, however, it can serve as a highly effective tool for diagnosing tendencies within families that impede growth toward a Christlike life, and for bringing health and wholeness to Christian families as well as to parishes. This systems approach is particularly effective insofar as it shifts the focus from individuals and particular issues to concentrate more broadly on the overall functioning of family and parish groups.

There is a tendency among some Orthodox Christians to embrace only Orthodox sources of wisdom. Much of modern science, however, derives from non-Orthodox sources. While it is vital to explore the compatibility of modern research and experience with Orthodox life and thought, it is just as crucial not to reject modern discoveries out of hand. With that in mind, we should note that one of the best resources for family systems theory and therapy as applied to parish life is Rabbi Edwin Friedman's book *Generation to Generation*.[6] A therapist who has offered his services to clergy of many faiths, Friedman describes in detail how parish families do and do not work effectively, and how they can be led toward healing.

Family systems therapy is equally applicable to individual parishes, since they typically function as family systems. To understand how this is true, and to explore particular parishes in terms of their generational family tree, we can ask questions such as the following: When was the parish founded, and under what circumstances? Who were the founders, and what were their ethnic and linguistic backgrounds? How well did they integrate into their new environment from the perspective of education, work, language, customs, social class, attachments to family, and roles within the community? Of which generation are the current members of the parish? What are their attitudes toward work, money, authority, the role of the clergy and clergy wives, the parish council, and their own roles within the community? An exploration of intergenerational dynamics that begins with questions like these can be especially helpful for

[6]E. Friedman, *Generation to Generation* (New York: Guilford, 1985).

Orthodox parishes that are dealing with their historical and cultural legacies as they attempt to integrate appropriately into contemporary American life.

Components of the Family System

Examining a few basic aspects of family systems will help us understand their dynamics. Specifically, and very briefly, we will consider (1) emotional distance, (2) triangulation, (3) family roles, (4) family rules, (5) the "identified patient" or symptom bearer, and (6) homeostasis.

Emotional distance refers to the degree of emotional separation or closeness within families. The continuum of growth and development is intimately connected to and dependent on emotional distance. Infants require emotional closeness in the form of nurturing and loving physical contact. As children grow, autonomy and independence become increasingly important. At a later stage, children require a healthy and balanced, yet flexible, interdependence. Partners in marriage go through various stages in their relationship, often maturing from an initial period of fusion, in which boundaries between spouses are blurred, to one of greater personal independence. Often spouses will attempt to use geographical distance to solve emotional problems. The ability to regulate emotional distance with others often comes down to the capacity to define oneself in a relationship. Flexibility is the key: maintaining different distances at different times, according to the needs of each partner or each member of the family unit. Easy and effective modes of communication, together with free expression of feelings, are essential for discovering and preserving appropriate emotional distance.

Triangulation refers to a dysfunctional strategy of communication. In Friedman's words, "When any two parts of a system become uncomfortable with one another, they will triangle in or focus upon a third person, or issue, as a way of stabilizing their own relationship with one another."[7] When a divorced couple approaches the time of their child's wedding, for example, the parents and children all experience a certain level of discomfort. The bride may prefer that her older brother walk her down the aisle so as not to hurt her mother's feelings by asking her estranged father to play that role. To deal with the conflicting emotions provoked by the situation, the triangulating bride avoids speaking to her father directly. Rather, she approaches the pastor with a request that he transmit her message to the parties concerned. By bringing the pastor in as a third party, she avoids confrontation with her father, and the triangulation is complete.

Family roles are familiar to all of us. We have all heard, for example, of the "black sheep of the family." This is usually a member who has not followed the established family rules. Or it could be someone who has brought shame to the family and has consequently been rejected by its other members. The "rich uncle," on the other hand, is the family member who provides financial support to others in the system, offering such things as money for education or medical care. Each plays a central family role: the black sheep through being rejected, the rich uncle through being accepted.

In addition to roles, families have *rules*, whether spoken or unspoken. A typical rule for most families is, "Don't air the dirty

[7]Ibid., 35.

laundry!" This is a way of saying that all families have secrets that if made public would tarnish their image. Many of these family rules are unconsciously passed down from one generation to the next.

The *symptom bearer* or *identified patient* is the member of the family who manifests signs of stress or pathology that characterize the entire system. In most families, this is a child who acts out family conflict by wetting the bed, failing in school, becoming involved with drugs or alcohol, becoming pregnant, or being hyperactive and disruptive. Other members of the family can ignore their own responsibility for collective stress, that is, ignore their own dysfunction, by laying blame on the identified patient. It is he or she who bears the symptoms and manifests the dysfunction of the entire family. Resolution of the problem, therefore, requires intervening in the whole family dynamic rather than focusing solely on the behavior of one of its members.

The entire spectrum of family dynamics is marked by a healthy or unhealthy quest for *homeostasis*. In a healthy family, the members have a secure sense of belonging to the group, while they receive appropriate support in forging their personal identities. Here there is encouragement of open expression and shared feelings. Trust is an integral part of a healthy family system, making possible change without crisis. An unhealthy system, on the other hand, is characterized by a focus on an identified patient and by resistance to change. By identifying one family member as the cause of everyone else's problems, the family remains in a state of homeostasis, although it is unhealthy and potentially destructive.

The Addictive Family System

Families affected by addiction live out these same family dynamics in particularly dysfunctional ways. They achieve their unhealthy homeostasis or equilibrium by adopting a number of classic roles and rules.

There are three basic rules common to all addictive family systems: "Don't talk!" "Don't trust!" "Don't feel!" Secrets are an integral part of such a system because secrets are symptomatic of the addict's condition and of the disease itself. Once a family secret is divulged and the truth comes out, trust is eroded among the family members. However much nonaddicted members may want to live in an environment built on trust, they cannot. They have too often been hurt by betrayal.

In an addictive family system, children learn early on that they are not allowed to express themselves freely. Generally it is only the addict in the family who claims that right. The children are brought up never to discuss with anyone, including other family members, what happens in the home. As a result, they become increasingly isolated both within and outside the family. They cannot bring other children home, for example, because it's too dangerous. They might be shamed by a parent's dysfunctional behavior, such as drunkenness, outbursts of anger, inappropriate joking, or physical violence.

The parents in an addictive family usually fail to validate their children's feelings. The atmosphere of the home is one of perpetual crisis and chaos. The addict usurps the right to express feelings and does so with anger or withdrawal (passive aggression). That anger is usually directed toward other family members and is accompanied by messages that convey both blame ("You are guilty; you made the mistake!") and shame ("You are worthless; you *are* the mistake!").

In such a situation, family roles are remarkably predictable. The spouse and children of the addict tend to become enablers; they facilitate or accommodate the addiction and the addict's behavior in order to retain a modicum of peace within the home. The role of the enabler is to allow (enable) the addict to continue in their addictive behavior by tolerating what is in fact intolerable conduct. Enablers tend also to wrap themselves up in denial. They just don't want to believe it's "that bad."

Within family systems, the children of the household tend to adopt specific and clearly defined roles. Typically, the first child adopts the role of "hero." He or she is the responsible one who overfunctions and overachieves in order to maintain the required homeostasis, the balance the family needs to go on functioning without changing in any radical way. While this child may receive praise for various achievements, he rarely receives affirmation, the sense that he is truly appreciated. Pushed toward ever more heroic accomplishments (assuming the functions abdicated by the parents, for example, or excelling in school), this child experiences a deep-seated sense of inadequacy. This in turn presses him toward still greater achievements. Here we have all the makings of a perfectionist. The successes of this "heroic child" serve to cover the family's shame. Outwardly, the child becomes the source of family satisfaction and pride. On the inside, however, he tends to be lonely, confused, and depressed. He takes the dysfunction of his parents or siblings upon himself and thereby carries the family's guilt.

A second child arrives in such a family and finds that the place of approval is already taken by the older sibling. To find her own place in the system, this child tends to seek attention through negative means, by acting out. Thus the child becomes the family "scapegoat." This is the one who usually becomes the identified patient. She hides, more or less effectively, feelings of anger, grief, a sense of abandonment, and alienation from the family group. The core feeling of such children is profound hurt. And in many cases, they end up in trouble with the law.

When the third child is born into this dysfunctional system, the addiction has progressed. Acutely aware of the chaos that reigns in the household, this child attempts to hide by taking a low profile. This is the role of the so-called "lost child," which is characterized by silence and grief. His main feelings are loneliness and depression, sometimes to the point that he becomes suicidal.

A fourth child who arrives in the midst of such a family discovers that most of the roles have been taken by her older siblings. The atmosphere is so heavy and depressing, this child tends to seek relief from the intensity of the family drama. The most frequent role the child assumes, therefore, is that of the "mascot" or "family clown." This is the comic, who relieves tension by using humor to diffuse potentially hazardous emotional and physical stresses among other family members. Apparently lighthearted and full of fun, she also becomes dysfunctional, bearing inside a heavy burden of fear and pain.

These roles are not necessarily permanent, nor are they exclusive. The hero can also be a mascot, just as a lost child can become a scapegoat. As older siblings leave the home to establish themselves elsewhere, the children left behind tend to shift roles in an attempt to maintain the desperately needed family homeostasis.

The result of these pressures is to ensnare each member of the family in codependency, which is itself an addiction. Those who live close to an addict adopt behaviors that are similar to or complementary to his. Codependents may become addicts themselves, seeking in the use of chemicals some way to medicate the pain they experience living in an addictive family. Others will develop psychiatric disorders. All of them, in any case, will be affected by depression, and many develop somatic disorders.

As grim as these scenarios and codependency may sound and actually be, we need always to remember that recovery is possible. Before we turn to various means for recovery, however, it would be useful to look more closely at specific addictions, including their characteristics and consequences.

Examples of Addictions

Alcoholism and Drug Addiction

Alcoholism and drug addiction often begin surreptitiously. A social drinker may cross the line into full-blown addiction without realizing it. A person taking prescribed tranquilizers begins to adjust dosages, then to visit other doctors and pharmacies to avoid detection. Adolescents are particularly vulnerable to pressures that lead to addiction. Illicit drugs (cocaine, marijuana, or ecstasy, for example) are innocuously labeled "recreational," and people both young and old are lulled into believing such drugs are not addictive.

Jean and Jimmy were little children, eight and nine respectively, when they used to "clean up" after their parents' cocktail parties. Going from table to table, they finished off the alcohol left in the glasses. By the time they were thirteen and fourteen, they were addicted. After she became addicted to marijuana and heroin as well, Jean died in her thirties, a victim of suicide. Jimmy became a career alcoholic, bearing his affliction for some forty-seven years. Now in his fifties, he is sober and in recovery, trying to learn skills, both social and occupational, that he normally would have learned in his adolescence.

What we usually see in the first stages of alcoholism seems innocuous enough: the urgency of that first drink of the day, occasional drinking to medicate feelings, and a gnawing sense of guilt. Very quickly tolerance develops, and the addict needs more of his drug of choice to achieve the same effect, to reach the same high. Jimmy, for example, at nine years old could achieve a high on just half a glass of beer. By the time he was thirteen, he needed two beers to feel tipsy and four to get drunk. He began having blackouts, chemically induced states of amnesia. (Although a person does not actually lose consciousness with blackouts, he or she is unable to remember what occurred while under the influence. Jean would find unfamiliar things in her coat pocket: a train ticket to Washington, D.C., or a used syringe. She had no idea how they had gotten there.)

As people move to the second stage of alcoholism, they tend to adopt grandiose and aggressive behavior. When they are hungover, they are moody and irritable. They begin to avoid friends and family, becoming more and more isolated. Any attempts by others to control their drinking fail, since they refuse to admit or even to discuss the problem. They regularly break promises and experience regret over many of their actions, all of which indicates an increasing pattern of moral deterioration.

In the late stage of alcoholism, people just can't stop drinking. They develop detoxification symptoms of shakes, sweats, and seizures, while they neglect food and basic physical care. Their lives become increasingly unmanageable, marked by legal problems, poor work performance, money troubles, and family disintegration.

It is often said that alcohol is a solvent, capable of dissolving marriages, work contracts, car keys, bank accounts, physical health, and spiritual values. The end station for many alcoholics is predictable: car crashes and other accidents, physical collapse or other serious health issues, psychiatric disorders, homicide, suicide, jail.

This tragic picture can take shape over a period of fifteen to twenty years from the onset of drinking. For drug addicts, the final stage comes more quickly. A cocaine addict, for instance, can bottom out in six months, taking their entire savings as well as their mental, physical, and spiritual health with them. When he was twenty-six years old, Phil received a $70,000 inheritance from his aunt. In the space of one summer, he spent every bit of it on his cocaine habit. By September, he was so emaciated that his condition finally broke through his parents' denial. They brought him to the emergency room, where the doctor told them Phil would not have lasted another week. After a short hospitalization, he was transferred to a drug rehabilitation center, where he spent a month getting clean. His greatest regret, he relates, was having to give up his white sports car, his favorite place to do lines of cocaine.

To support their habit, many drug addicts become involved in the sale of drugs, in prostitution, and in other illegal behavior. If they are parents, they seriously endanger their children and often lose them to the foster care system. As addicts become increasingly enslaved to their addictions, their families develop the disease of codependency in an effort to maintain homeostasis and control the addicts' erratic and destructive ways of acting out.

Codependency

There are many definitions of codependency. Family therapist and author Robert Subby writes that codependency is "an emotional, psychological, and behavioral condition that develops as a result of an individual's prolonged exposure to and practice of a set of oppressive rules which prevent the open expression of feeling as well as the direct discussion of personal and interpersonal problems."[8] Many people describe themselves, relative to the addict, as "caretakers" or "fixers." Ann Smith, a specialist in the field of addictions, describes codependency as "a pattern of painful dependence on compulsive behaviors and on approval seeking in an attempt to gain safety, identity and self worth."[9] This painful dependence on compulsive behaviors is itself an

[8]R. Subby, in Sharon Wegscheider–Cruse, ed., *Codependency: An Emerging Issue* (Pompano Beach, FL: Health Communications, 1984).

[9]A. W. Smith, workshops. See her *Grandchildren of Alcoholics: Another Generation of Co-dependency* (Pompano Beach, FL: Health Communications, 1988).

addiction, which explains why we need to consider codependency in this chapter. People who live with and work around addicts have a tendency to develop codependency, unless they attempt to counteract the negative influences of the addict's behavior by going into a program of recovery such as a Twelve Step support group.

Like all addictions, codependency erodes a person's spiritual life. God calls us to find our identity, safety, and self-worth in him, and to be dependent on him in a healthy and holy manner. Codependents, however, seek security in people, things, and situations that are unfulfilling and often harmful. Symptoms of the codependent family system include chaos and an ongoing state of crisis. Codependents, like alcoholics, will create a crisis atmosphere if one does not already exist. This serves to focus everyone in the family system away from their true feelings, producing a state of numbness. In this way, homeostasis is preserved, since no one is sufficiently motivated to introduce change into the system.

Codependency almost always involves some form of enabling behavior. This means that the codependent person puts a great deal of energy into maintaining an environment that removes or minimizes the consequences and pain of another person's addictive behavior. This makes it easier for addicts to continue their dysfunctional patterns of thinking and acting.

Enablers tend to minimize the effects of addiction by apologizing for the addict: "It isn't that bad." "He didn't mean it." They also rationalize: "She behaved that way only because she cares about you." In other words, enablers are master excuse-makers and cover-up artists. A wife, for example, might phone her husband's boss and spin a lie to explain her spouse's absenteeism, tardiness, or inability to complete a task in the time allotted for it.

How can we distinguish enabling from healthy compassion? True compassion is grounded in love, based on Christ's teaching to feed the hungry, clothe the naked, visit those in prison, heal the sick, give to the needy (Mt 25.35ff). Its fruits are compatible with those of the Holy Spirit (Gal 5.22–23). While enabling behavior may originate in compassion and love, it actually facilitates the addicted person in their addiction. The fruits of enabling behavior are those associated with the progressive nature of addictions. Examples of enabling are loaning money to a compulsive gambler, buying alcohol for an alcoholic, or ordaining a known religious or sexual addict to the priesthood.

When we choose true compassion over enabling, we open our lives and the lives of those we are trying to help to an experience of grace. By "speaking the truth in love," we can offer a gift that becomes the catalyst for the addict's healing. Yet we need to be aware that it can also provoke, at least for a time, a situation of conflict.

In the long run, the moral fiber of the enabler becomes compromised, because he tells lies, lives lies, and makes others feel comfortable believing lies. In his misguided attempt to make things better, the enabler merely perpetuates the addict's unhealthy behavior.

Workaholism

Work addiction is particularly insidious because it is a "clean" addiction. It is not only socially acceptable; it is highly encouraged—in schools, in the workplace, and in the Church. In the corporate world, CEOs tend to push employees into workaholism, requiring average workweeks of fifty to eighty hours. Schools bless workaholic students with scholarships, and universities reward them with everything from early acceptance to Phi Beta Kappa keys. Priests and pastors often burn out because unspoken expectations both from hierarchs and parish councils pressure them into addictive patterns of activity, playing on their sense of guilt when they don't measure up. Even on the home front, workaholism is rampant. Housewives compulsively keep busy to the point that their lives are ruled by stress and fatigue.

Yet work is a necessary component of everyone's life (Gen 3.17–19). How, then, are we to know when work has become addictive?

Certain symptoms or characteristics offer significant clues. Workaholics rarely ask for help and spend large amounts of time preoccupied with their current activity. They are caught up in a dual sense of urgency and frustration. "There is never enough time," because the addict is constantly setting unrealistic deadlines. Multitasking is a hallmark of workaholism. Simultaneously talking on a cell phone, purchasing something in a store, and writing a memo seems perfectly normal to the workaholic.

Work addicts are plagued by perfectionism. From childhood they have learned that the only passing grade is an A, and therefore every result, every achievement, must be perfect and flawless. Otherwise, they have failed. Each project they undertake requires an inordinate amount of time and energy. It becomes their sole focus, thereby eliminating family gatherings, socializing with friends, and just relaxing. On a workaholic's list of priorities, personal needs come last. As a result, work addiction often leads to health crises, sleep disorders, and depression.

Workaholism afflicts individuals, institutions, organizations, and even churches. In a workaholic environment, the person who attempts to live in a balanced and healthy way will be criticized for not doing enough. They will be made to feel ashamed and guilty. In one religious institution, the faculty and staff gathered to review the job description of each person, based on their actual performance. The intention was to reduce the level of stress within the institution by decreasing each one's workload to manageable proportions. But because everyone was mired in workaholism, the meeting actually served to identify the many unassigned tasks that still needed to be done. This extra load was then parceled out to the already overburdened individuals who had gathered looking for some respite. Many of them left the meeting bemused, angry, or desperate.

The workaholic will stay late on the job, go in early, work on weekends, accept double shifts and duty on holidays, and take on special projects with unrealistic deadlines. Because the workaholic is not able to meet needs in an intimate relationship, the spouse tends to lose himself or herself in a similar pattern of behavior. A wife, for example, will become overly involved in social events or attempt to micromanage the lives of her children. For their part, the children in such a family experience an immense void, since they have no one they can rely on to meet their normal emotional needs. The work addict can always justify the addiction by pointing to the need for extra income. The potential results of this behavior are no different from the outcome of other addictions: depression, divorce, and in some cases, suicide.

Rigid expectations, coupled with obsessive-compulsive tendencies, fuel the workaholic's addiction. They are rewarded ("stroked") by praise, pay raises, and promotions, each of which serves to reinforce the choice to overwork to the point of burnout. When the workaholic is a priest or pastor, the parish members often feel the results of his addiction in his attempts to control all that goes on in the community. He and they together fall into a kind of bondage. Once again, the gospel of Christ has another message. "It was for freedom that Christ set us free," St Paul declares. "Therefore, keep standing firm and do not be subject again to a yoke of slavery" (Gal 5.1).

Sexual Addiction

Ken, Tania, and their two children were just sitting down for supper when the doorbell rang. Tania got up to answer. The color drained from her face when she saw the two policemen. They asked for her husband. "Is anything wrong?" she asked. The officers went into the dining room, told Ken to stand up, handcuffed him, and read him his rights. He had been accused of online solicitation of underage girls. One of the officers asked for his computer. They left, Ken and computer in tow, Tania and the kids in shock. As the case unraveled, Tania learned that Ken had been a sex addict from his teen years, when an adult family friend had supplied him with pornographic magazines.

With the advent of the Internet and on-demand cable TV, cybersex has invaded the homes, hotel rooms, and workplaces of America. The immediate availability of the Internet, coupled with the presumed anonymity of its use, has served to swell the numbers of those who are sexually addicted. The Internet's interactive capabilities, while enhancing access to information, also serve sexual predators in search of unsuspecting victims.

Sexual addiction is a disease of levels. Patrick Carnes, in *Out of the Shadows*, describes these levels of behavior and the addict's belief system.[10] At level 1, sexual addiction can include masturbation, pornography, prostitution, and compulsive heterosexual or homosexual relationships. Level 2 includes exhibitionism, voyeurism, indecent phone calls, and indecent liberties (such as using a hidden camera to film a toilet booth, filming up a woman's skirt, or "feeling" in a crowd). At level 3, sexual misconduct includes child molestation, incest, and rape.

Core beliefs, in Carnes's analysis, have to do with self-image, relationships, personal needs, and sexuality. In dysfunctional cases, they include the conviction that "I am basically a bad, unworthy person, and no one would love me as I am." Although addicts experience sex as their most important need, they are convinced that they cannot depend on others to meet and satisfy it. Trapped in their world of excessive need, they try to resolve the tension in unhealthy ways. Attempting to avoid painful feelings, their behavior in fact increases feelings of shame.

Many persons addicted to sex are victims of childhood sexual abuse. They have been emotionally abandoned and perpetuate the cycle by abandoning themselves. They often engage in harmful activity or make harmful choices, such as missing work in order to seek out prostitutes or other sources of sexual stimulation. The

---

[10] P. Carnes, *Out of the Shadows: Understanding Sexual Addiction* (Minneapolis: CompCare, 1983), 23–61. See also his *A Gentle Path through the Twelve Steps* (Minneapolis: CompCare, 1993).

result is usually a breakdown in family relationships due to conflict, financial problems, and alienation.

A cautionary note needs to be sounded about self-help groups for those with sexual addictions. Many of these groups allow various forms of sexual activity outside the framework of a traditional marriage. This works against any real healing process. The one self-help group that is appropriate for Orthodox Christians is Sexaholics Anonymous, which allows for sexual activity only between spouses in a monogamous, heterosexual conjugal union.

Religiosity

Religious addictions, like all other addictions, are progressive and chronic. In the early stages, the addict typically engages in frequent Bible reading and church attendance in order to calm feelings and lessen anxiety. One could reply that many perfectly normal people attend church often and read the Bible "religiously." Religious addicts, however, attend church and read Scripture compulsively, and they experience a great deal of anxiety when they are unable to maintain those behaviors.

In the middle stage, the religious addict makes moral judgments that reflect on others while they damage himself. For example, he will often view any sexual activity as dirty and unacceptable. He neglects normal family and professional activities in favor of some religious duty or service. Then again, the addict tends to transfer guilt and shame to all those who do not believe as he does. A typical tactic in transferring shame is to invoke what is pleasing or not pleasing to God: "Anything other than X (whatever I want, feel, need, or believe) is not worthy of God." Religion thus becomes a tool for manipulation. This goes hand in hand with a refusal to discuss any issue that might lead the addict to change his mind or alter his convictions.

In the late stage of religious addiction, the obsession leads to psychiatric disorders, financial losses (due to immoderate giving to religious causes), and to decisions that disrupt family life and jeopardize the family's well being. Such decisions include going off on missionary trips or religious pilgrimages, abandoning the family in the process. Father Leo Booth, who has long worked with victims of religious addiction, holds that this affliction "keeps people chained in superstitions, in ignorance, and in hypocrisy."[11]

In addition to the addictions we have outlined here, there are many others that we often don't recognize. Among them are nicotine and caffeine addictions, compulsive shopping and shoplifting, bulimia and anorexia, "working out" to extremes, and engaging in high-risk sports for the high they produce. Generally speaking, any substance or behavior can become the source of addiction. All addictions exhibit progression through stages, ending in sickness and heartbreak for the victim and all the codependents around him. Everyone within the addict's social network is affected; therefore, to some degree, everyone needs treatment.

[11]L. Booth, *Breaking the Chains: Understanding Religious Addiction and Religious Abuse* (Longbeach, CA: Emmaus Publications, 1989), 65.

Trauma and Addiction

Many people turn to potentially addictive behaviors as a means of covering the pain of past traumas. Life events are often overwhelming, and they can render people helpless in the face of uncontrollable circumstances. The effects of trauma are inscribed in the body and the brain. Memory and emotions are deeply affected, and they can recycle traumatic feelings into the present whenever an experience similar to or a sensory memory of the original trauma occurs (smells, sights, tastes, sounds, tactile sensations). Even the calendar can trigger a full-blown response to a trauma, as it recalls the date on which that event occurred. The ACOA (Adult Children of Alcoholics) movement, which began in the 1970s, highlighted the role of trauma in addicted families. Many of the adult children of those families suffer from PTSD (post-traumatic stress disorder), manifesting symptoms not unlike those of soldiers who return from a war zone.[12]

In effect, families affected by addiction *are* war zones. Jeffrey's first memory was of looking up to see his father smash through a plate glass door to grab his mother. She had become the object of his father's drunken, violent rage. An older sibling intervened to break up the fight, and the younger children escaped to safety. Jeffrey was four years old at the time. To this day, any hint of conflict raises for him a code-red alert, including the same physiological responses provoked by the original trauma.

---

[12]See Janet Woititz, *Adult Children of Alcoholics* (Pompano Beach, FL: Health Communications, 1983). This classic work is still available at most major bookstores.

When trauma and loss are at the root of addictions, they must be treated as well. Otherwise, relapse is almost inevitable. The therapeutic technique known as psychodrama[13] can be an effective tool for healing trauma, because it targets emotions and thoughts simultaneously in the context of the recreated experience. A newly created psychodrama scene offers a solution for healing and role training to prepare the person for future healthy behavior. Other trauma-reduction techniques, such as EMDR (eye-movement desensitization and reprocessing), can also prove effective. Then again, group therapy can be a critical aid in healing the disordered relationships that so often mark the lives of adult children of alcoholics and other trauma survivors.

Defining the Solution: Recovery

What Is Recovery?

In Christian terms, recovery refers to the rediscovery and refurbishing of the divine image in which we were all created. It consists of a lengthy pilgrimage that leads us to identify all that is not of God, and to make new, healthy, and holy choices in our lives. It implies that we need to begin anew in order to change our understanding of who we are and to assume healthier patterns of behavior. This usually requires the help of other people, trained professionals who can guide the process toward healing with intelligence, sensitivity, and compassion. In some cases, that guidance

---

[13]Psychodrama is a therapeutic technique originated by the late psychiatrist J. L. Moreno and further developed by his widow, Zerka Moreno. It is a useful and highly effective method that is increasingly known and used in the United States and throughout the world.

may take the form of a planned intervention, a process by which help is offered to someone who is in the grip of addiction. It is a highly successful means of engaging the addicted person in recovery. Vernon Johnson's book *I'll Quit Tomorrow*[14] details the intervention process, which is similar for all types of addictions. Counselors who specialize in addictions are available through the Yellow Pages or the referral network of Alcoholics Anonymous.

Treatment

Treatment is the means through which recovery is possible. The first step toward treatment is abstinence. This requires that the addicted person stop using all addictive substances and cease all addictive behaviors. A monitoring system, which may include random urine samples and "breathalyzers," along with behavioral observation by competent staff members, determines whether progress is being made.

Treatment takes many forms: in-patient rehabilitation programs (from several weeks to months in duration, including detoxification when needed), halfway houses (intended to provide a supportive, abstinent community after the patient is discharged from an in-patient facility), intensive out-patient rehabilitation programs (usually an evening program for sixteen hours a week), less intensive regular addictions counseling on an out-patient basis, and Twelve Step self-help support groups. Treatment of the family members is an integral part of most programs. Reconciliation among family members is an important part of the recovery

[14]V. Johnson, *I'll Quit Tomorrow* (San Francisco: Harper and Row, 1980), esp. 48–61.

process, in that it addresses the accumulated hurt, anger, fear, shame, and grief of all those involved. Effective treatment will be individually tailored to the specific stage of recovery of each person. A treatment plan outlines objectives along with an anticipated timeline for their achievement.

Most treatment plans include referral to Twelve Step programs. These programs, which are free of charge, exist worldwide. They invite people to share their experience, strength, and hope, to accept the guidance of a sponsor (a peer with more recovery experience), and to "work the steps." Programs of this kind include Cocaine Anonymous, Narcotics Anonymous, Codependents Anonymous, Overeaters Anonymous, Adult Children of Alcoholics, Kleptomaniacs and Shoplifters Anonymous, Emotions Anonymous, and many others. Al-Anon was founded as a support group for spouses and other family members of alcoholics, as Alateen was for adolescents. Al-Anon, Alateen, Adult Children of Alcoholics, and Codependents Anonymous all target the inevitable codependency that develops in the lives of persons who have close contact with addicts.

While hospitals offer crisis management in cases of addictions (dealing with overdose, detoxification, etc.) and provide medical treatment for physical symptoms, they usually do not address long-term recovery needs in the areas of spirituality and psychoeducation. This can be confusing both for addicts and their families, who often believe that the addict has already received all necessary treatment during a hospitalization. A well-rounded treatment program, however, will focus on three complementary aspects of the healing process: medical, psychoeducational, and spiritual.

Relapse is a common part of recovery, because addicts have so much to learn and so many old habits to overcome. To help avoid relapse, addicted persons need to modify their personal relationships, especially those which involve codependency. People, places, or things that merely fostered the addiction need to be eliminated from addicts' lives altogether. For example, a person in recovery must have absolutely no contact with dealers or former friends who supplied drugs; if a paycheck served as a trigger for buying alcohol or for gambling, the money should be deposited automatically into a bank account; and sex addicts should get rid of all pornography and install a filter on any computer to which they have access. Even persons with the best of intentions can relapse during the healing process. About half of those who do relapse get back into recovery, while the other half return to their former, dysfunctional patterns of behavior. Addicts in recovery may also switch addictions, giving themselves over to another compulsion.

Treatment resources can be found online and in the Yellow Pages. You may call an addictions counselor or the help line in your area. You can also find online lists of rehabilitation programs nationwide. Bookstores are also a good source of information.

An essential part of treatment is the aftercare plan for both the addicted person and his or her family members. People are likely to relapse if they do not follow through with their aftercare plans. If they do relapse, the new situation is even more difficult to deal with, since the person can now claim that he or she has been to treatment and has learned all there is to know. The person falls again into denial, and the disease continues its devastating progression.

Addictions and Recovery within the Church

Addiction within the Church

Just as addictive nuclear families are plagued with denial, so too is the church family. Denial is a powerful defense mechanism that allows people to go through life without considering how their thoughts and actions are at odds with the call to holiness. This leads to a moral dilemma. As A. W. Schaef and Diane Fassel write in *The Addictive Organization,* "Ethical deterioration is the inevitable outcome of immersion in the addictive system. It is easy to understand how this happens. If your life is taken up by lying to yourself and others, attempting to control, perfectionism, denial, grabbing what you can for yourself, and refusing to let in information that would alter the addictive paradigm, then you are spiritually bankrupt."[15]

Just as in family systems, addicts assume roles within the parish. People do not want to admit that the priest or choir leader could be an alcoholic, drug addict, compulsive gambler, or sex addict, although they tend to applaud their workaholism and perfectionism.

In one area with a high rate of alcoholism, priests attempted to control the abuse in their communities by the pledge system. As people with a drinking problem came to confession, they were asked to sign a statement, promising they would no longer drink. No accompanying treatment was offered, however, because the priests mistakenly believed that sobriety is a matter of willpower. They were not aware that addiction is a disease that can be healed

[15]A. W. Schaef and Diane Fassel, *The Addictive Organization* (San Francisco: Harper, 1990), 67.

only through a therapeutic recovery process involving mind, body, and spirit. As a result, the pledge system failed. Church members went back to drinking, now with the added burden of shame and guilt caused by the Church's condemnation.

Examples of denial are found among the Orthodox, just as they are in virtually all religious organizations, Christian or not. Several years ago, a committee was formed to investigate sexual abuse by clergy and to propose guidelines for dealing with the problem. Once it was learned that a member of the committee was himself engaged in sexual misconduct, the group was unofficially disbanded. The other committee members were never again contacted by anyone with regard to their work or possible future assignments. This is a perfect example of the addictive system's primary rule: "Don't talk!"

Enabling in churches takes the same form as enabling in families. One parish responded to its priest's arrest for driving while under the influence by getting him out of jail and making sure he went before a lenient judge. A seminary dean sent a student home, stating that he was suffering from extreme fatigue. In this way, he avoided dealing with the student's known use of cocaine. An alcoholic bishop was enabled to continue his addiction for years, simply because no one dared to confront him. He went into treatment only following a health crisis that led his doctor to intervene and make arrangements for appropriate treatment. All of these enabling behaviors prove to be destructive for everyone involved.

Monastic communities can also be caught up in addictions and dysfunctional family systems. Some who seek the monastic life grew up in alcoholic homes and never received treatment. They might arrive at the monastery with a deep and genuine spiritual longing, yet also hoping to acquire a sense of belonging and meaning. If the abbot or abbess rules autocratically or functions on an affective level as father or mother, they can foster infantilization in less stable and less mature members of the community. Then again, a significant number of monastics are trauma survivors. They do their utmost to lead a life of prayer, faithful to the monastic rule. Yet if they are burdened by acute losses that they were never able properly to grieve, their consequent dysfunctional behavior and attitudes affect each of their monastic brothers or sisters, just as they do among those in the world outside.

God's grace can penetrate the frozen depths of psychological and emotional woundedness that many people in the Church, including many of those in monastic orders, bear within themselves. True miracles of healing have occurred, either because of, or in spite of, a dysfunctional atmosphere. Nevertheless, a great deal of suffering is perpetuated in parishes, in seminaries, and in monastic communities by ignorance or denial. Because of these factors, persons who are caught up in that suffering often refuse to seek the help they so desperately need. Their denial takes the form of religious platitudes ("We are relying on God") or assertions that treatment for recovery from addictions "is not compatible with the monastic way" or is "not Orthodox." It is, of course, essential that we rely on God throughout the recovery process. And it is true that some forms of treatment are incompatible with the spiritual life. This matter requires discernment. What therapeutic process will help addicted people rediscover and give expression to the image of God that lies within the depths of their being? In fact, there are many such processes, including those proposed here.

Fortunately, monastic communities, seminaries, and parishes are slowly opening their doors to the appropriate assistance that is increasingly available to them. For that assistance to be effective, however, the church community must begin by recognizing and dealing responsibly with the addictions in its midst. It needs to admit that in purely human terms, it is powerless to deal with these dysfunctional and destructive patterns of behavior. Seeking the power and grace of God through the guidance and prayer of spiritual fathers and mothers, together with effective medical and psychological therapy, the parish community can then begin to grow toward genuine and lasting healing.

The Recovery-Oriented Church

Throughout this chapter, I have repeatedly insisted that recovery from addiction is possible. This is as true for the church community as it is for the nuclear or extended family.

For those preparing to enter the priesthood, seminary is the appropriate place to acquire basic information about addictions. The screening of seminary candidates (background checks and psychological evaluations), already practiced at some Orthodox theological schools, is a crucial element in helping to eliminate those who are addicted or who have psychiatric disorders that are incompatible with the priesthood.

A comprehensive seminary program in the area of addictions could provide both clergy and lay leaders with a means for creating recovery resource networks in their communities. Visiting treatment facilities and becoming acquainted with clinicians will not only facilitate a team approach but will also allow for referrals to be based on appropriate knowledge and experience. In particular, it is vital to become familiar with the Twelve Step self-help network. The most effective way to understand these programs is through firsthand experience. Some Orthodox churches have actually founded their own Twelve Step recovery programs.

Increasingly, an Employee/Student Assistance Program is available in many jurisdictions for clergy, seminarians, and their families. This service offers assessments and referrals and is confidential and free of charge.

A healthy church will develop appropriate guidelines and policies regarding substance abuse and addictive behaviors, as has already been done in several of our jurisdictions. Parishes will be designated as drug-free zones. When alcohol is served as part of a liturgical function, as is the case after Holy Saturday liturgy, then water or juice should also be available not only for children but also for recovering alcoholics. Bars should have no place in our churches. Supervision at all parish events should be mandatory. This includes supervision of children who serve at the altar, where wine is available.

When problems do occur within a parish community, they need to be addressed immediately. This is particularly true of sexual misconduct within churches, seminaries, and monasteries. Our various jurisdictions have published guidelines regarding sexual misconduct, and these should be posted and made available in brochures that people can take home and study. Perpetrators, victims, and their families, together with the entire community, are in need of healing when sexual misconduct does occur.[16]

[16]N. Hopkins and M. Laaser, *Restoring the Soul of a Church* (Collegeville, MN: Liturgical Press, 1995).

To date, a significant number of people who were sexually abused in church settings have been revictimized by the Church when ecclesiastical lawyers have advised hierarchs to have no contact with those bringing the allegations. In some cases, victims of sexual abuse and their families have resorted to lawsuits to seek restitution, although for the most part, they would have been content to receive from a bishop or priest an acknowledgment of the abuse (validation), together with sufficient monetary assistance to cover the costs of therapy. It is standard procedure to require a gag order for victims who settle with the Church out of court. This practice not only reinforces the "don't talk" rule; it also perpetuates a sense of shame and abandonment in victims and their families.

As a result of these pressures—denial, enabling, codependency—the local church, like the family, can become an unsafe place, unwilling to break the silence, unwilling to take steps toward developing educational tools and policies needed to minister adequately and faithfully to those with addictions in its midst.

A recovery-oriented church is willing to establish an open dialogue on any subject that affects its members. It is concerned to protect its children, whatever the cost, by establishing and implementing policies that ensure the safety of all. A recovery-oriented church is proactive in the domain of education and prevention on all topics relating to addictions.

In Orthodox Christian tradition, the role of a healthy, well-informed, compassionate spiritual father or mother is vital. If this one person in the addict's life has the wisdom and courage to confront their spiritual child with the truth, gently yet firmly, guiding him or her through their fear and on to appropriate treatment, extraordinary healing could result.

Scripture declares "the truth will set you free." Getting to the truth is often a painful process. Many Twelve Step programs use this affirmation, but they add an important caveat: "The truth will set you free, but first it will make you miserable." This is particularly true of addictions and addictive behavior. Perhaps this temporary misery is the price that we and our churches have to pay in order to become healthy, to be truly founded on the teachings of Christ, and to be open to healing and growth.

For those who embrace recovery, there is the possibility of giving up addictive behaviors, identifying the dysfunctional rules and roles they may have adopted over the years, and making new life choices compatible with health and holiness.

For people who have been in denial, the information provided in this chapter may cause a certain amount of hurt, anger, and pain. It can be extremely difficult to confront the truth about ourselves and those we love, and to take the necessary steps to achieve healing. Yet we each need to make this courageous effort as individuals, as families, and as members of the body of Christ.

The pathway to recovery is essentially spiritual. However effective particular therapeutic approaches may be, they will ultimately fail if the person is not healed at the level of spirit, mind, and heart. From the perspective and experience of Orthodox

Christianity, we recognize that prayer is an integral part of the healing process, as are the sacraments of confession, communion, and unction. In and through the entire recovery process, we can draw strength, hope, and healing grace from Jesus Christ, who is the same yesterday, today, and forever. Jesus promised that at his second coming, he would wipe away every tear from our eyes (Rev 21.4). As we await this eschatological blessing, we are called to undertake intense preparation in our own lives and in the lives of our families, our neighbors, and our church communities. That preparation includes healing from addictions, a healing worked out ultimately by the Spirit of God who dwells within us.

We need to embrace our true calling with boldness and with a genuine desire for holiness. To the extent that we do so, we have every reason to expect that our lives will be filled with peace, thanksgiving, and joy. That joy is incarnational. Its true source is Christ himself, who entered into our world and took on himself our human nature in order to open before us the pathway to salvation and eternal life. Christ is the light of the world. It is he who invites us to be healed and who shows us the way out of the darkness of addiction. This unfettering from compulsive behaviors leads to true freedom, a freedom each of us can embrace for ourselves and as members of the Christian community.

Once we achieve that liberty, we can grow, in the power and grace of Christ, toward a life that is truly moral and truly holy. In that freedom, we can allow the Spirit to work within us a transformation from a fallen and broken image to the divine image in which we were created. Thereby we will reflect ever more fully the beauty and glory of that image, to ourselves and to those around us, as God and all the angels in heaven rejoice.

chapter six

THE HOPE OF GLORY: FROM A PHYSICAL TO A SPIRITUAL BODY

Christ in you, the hope of glory

—Colossians 1.27

At this point, we turn to a difficult yet crucial subject that concerns each of us in the most direct and personal way: the "mystery of death." This is an especially timely topic, since the conflict and violence that so mark the world today force us to look perhaps more closely than ever before at the ultimate meaning of both our life and our death. War, terrorism, poverty, earthquakes, and epidemic illness, together with our personal vulnerabilities, take death out of the realm of the hypothetical and place it squarely in the context of our daily experience. From the morning headlines to tragic accidents and wasting diseases, we are constantly reminded of our mortality. These reminders oblige us to ask whether that mortality leaves our lives with any real transcendent meaning and value. The mystery of death, then, is a major element in any bioethical reflection on life.

In the next and final chapter of this book, we will turn to the way Orthodox spiritual tradition, informed by medical science, calls us to accompany those persons who have entered the terminal phase of their earthly existence. The aim of this present chapter is to set the stage for those more practical reflections by providing a theological grounding for our approach to death and the question of what appropriate care we can offer dying patients.

Since the topic is so vast, I would like to focus here on one of its most significant yet misunderstood aspects—the transition from what the apostle Paul calls the physical (literally the "psychic") body to the resurrected spiritual body, from the *sōma psychikon* to the *sōma pneumatikon* (1 Cor 15.44). From a pastoral as well as a theological perspective, it is important for us to understand this transition in order fully to hear the gospel proclamation. That proclamation, in brief, holds that the transition from our earthly existence to eternal life occurs in such a way as to preserve somatic (bodily) identity from one state to the other. Death, in other words, does not mean annihilation of our bodily existence, nor does it involve an entirely new creation. For those who die in Christ, death involves a transformation—a metamorphosis or rebirth—in continuity with our physical being, which preserves our distinctive personal identity and integrity while it fulfills within us and for us what the apostle terms "the hope of glory."

Body and Soul

In Orthodox pastoral practice, we have acquired the habit of praying, in cases of terminal illness, for the "peaceful separation of soul and body." This well-meaning formula could be problematic, as it might suggest that the human person is constituted of two fundamentally different elements: an earthly body and a

heavenly soul. This is not a biblical perspective. It is reflective of
the Platonic and Hellenistic dualism that conceives the body to be
the prison house of the soul, and redemption—or simply the phenomenon of physical death—to consist in the liberation of the
soul from the body, with the subsequent return of the soul to its
place of heavenly origin. Underlying this notion is the belief that
souls are preexistent, that they existed before our bodies were created. This kind of dualistic anthropology, represented for example by third-century Christian theologian Origen of Alexandria
(†254), was rejected by the great majority of early church fathers,
long before Origen's final condemnation at the Fifth Ecumenical
Council in 553 (if indeed his inclusion in the list of anathematized
heretics is not a later interpolation).

Already in the second Christian century, the apologists Justin
Martyr († ca. 165) and Tatian († ca. 160) posed the fundamental
question, Does Christian faith affirm the "immortality of the
soul," or the "resurrection of the body"? Let us look more closely
at each side of the question. Put simply, the notion of the immortality of the soul is based on the idea that only the physical body
is subject to death. The soul does not die; it is exempt from the
powers of death and corruption. The soul, in this view, is sometimes pictured as a divine spark that has its origin in God and for
a time becomes incarnate in a mortal human body. When that
body dies, the soul is released to return to the place of its divine
origin. Some of those who hold to the immortality of the soul also
see the soul as preexisting the body; others say it is created simultaneously with the body. But either way, the soul does not die.
Once the body has ceased to live, the soul simply passes on to
dwell with other souls in the kingdom of God.

"Resurrection of the body," on the other hand, means that the power of death (and in the Scriptures, death is indeed known to be a power) touches and affects every aspect of human existence, including the life of the soul. While the soul may be characterized as eternal or even immortal, it is nevertheless subject to death insofar as death tears apart the soul's psychosomatic unity with the body. In this perspective, soul is the life force or life principle that animates and sustains human existence in all its aspects, physical, mental, and spiritual. Death brings about the dissolution of the psychosomatic unity that constitutes the human person, a unity that will be reestablished only with the coming in glory of the Son of God and the universal resurrection. That momentous event, when the dead will "rise from their tombs at the Last Day" (cf. Jn 5.28–29; 11.24), will bring about a full reintegration of soul, mind, and spirit in a new somatic reality that is the resurrected spiritual body. Personal identity will be fully preserved, and God's work of creation and redemption will be brought to completion. "For as in Adam all die, so also in Christ shall all be made alive. . . . So it is with the resurrection of the dead. What is sown is perishable, what is raised is imperishable. . . . It is sown a physical body, it is raised a spiritual body" (1 Cor 15.22, 42–44).

Which of these views—immortality of the soul or resurrection of the body—did the early Christian apologists and other church fathers defend and preach? Clearly, it was the latter. "Immortality of the soul" distorts the Christian understanding of the meaning and value of the human body, while it undermines a biblical eschatology that sees resurrection of the body as the means by which we are able to participate in Christ's own resurrection and glorification.

Tatian, for example, declared, "The soul is not in itself immortal . . . but mortal. Yet it is possible for it not to die" (*Oratio ad Grecos*, 13). The greatest biblical theologian of the pre-Nicene period, St Irenaeus of Lyon († ca. 200), subsequently affirmed that the soul is not intrinsically immortal but is created by God and is granted life by God: "For just as the body animated by the soul is not itself the soul, but participates in the soul as long as God wills, in the same way the soul is not itself life, but rather it participates in the life that God grants to it" (*Against Heresies* 2.34.4).

To the present day, the Orthodox consensus holds that the soul is created simultaneously with the body. In today's language, we would say it is created at fertilization, when the nuclei of sperm and ovum unite to form the human zygote. As noted earlier, the unity of soul and body is so total that we can affirm not that we have or possess a soul but that the human person *is* soul. The created human being is ensouled existence, animated by the *nephesh* or life breath of God (cf. Gen 2.7). Soul, then, is the principle of animation, originating with God, who is the source of life. The soul is proper to the body; it is a constituent element of the body's composition. Once created, however, the soul is characterized by immortality in the sense that for those who live in Christ, it will not die but will be reintegrated into the transformed, spiritual body at the general resurrection. Thus St Irenaeus once again:

> We cannot speak of the "mortal soul," because the soul is the breath of life. . . . To die, in effect, is to lose the way of being that is proper to living things, to be without breath, without life, without movement, and to become dissolved into the elements from which we received the principle of our existence. This, however, cannot happen

to the soul, because it is the breath of life; nor can it happen to the spirit, because it is not complex but simple. . . . It is the flesh that experiences death. Once the soul has departed, the flesh is left without breath and without life; it dissolves little by little into the earth from which it was taken. Thus it is the flesh which is mortal.

—*Against Heresies* 5.7.1; cf. 13.3

To St Irenaeus and the entire Orthodox tradition, it is essential to distinguish between two key concepts: eternity and immortality. Eternity must not be thought of as an endless extension through time. Eternity is rather a quality of being, in ceaseless communion with God; thus the Johannine notion of eternal life, which begins in the present age and endures beyond death (cf. Jn 5.24). To say that the soul, the principle of life, is eternal, is to affirm that from its creation at conception, it possesses the capacity to animate the human creature from the beginning of his or her existence, and to dwell in permanent communion with God in the realm of his divine being, a communion that will endure beyond the limits of earthly existence. (This is why we can even now participate in the "eternal communion of saints," sharing with deceased holy people their glorification of God and asking them to intercede on our behalf. They are no longer in the flesh, but they are still characterized by ensouled existence. And that existence they share both with us and with God.) The doctrine of the immortality of the soul, on the other hand, implies that the soul is exempt from death, oblivion, or annihilation, because it is metaphysically distinct from the body and independent of it. According to this view, death has no power over the soul and ultimately does not affect it.

The human soul is not mortal, as is the flesh; the soul does not simply disappear with the irreversible cessation of cardiorespiratory functioning and subsequent "brain death." Yet the soul cannot be said to be immortal in the sense that it is exempt from the destructive power of death. At death, once again, the soul is tragically separated from its bodily or somatic reality. (*Tragically* because God created us for life, not for death.) The soul thus "dies," insofar as it inevitably succumbs to the devastating consequences of death: disintegration of the body's various constituent elements. The soul, nevertheless, is eternal, in the sense that it does not undergo the same dissolution as the flesh but continues to exist after the death of the flesh (which we habitually speak of in a confusing and rather misleading way as the physical body).

In this perspective, we can easily understand the Church's liturgical language, which declares that at death the soul "leaves" or is "separated from" the body, even if that language can be misleading. (More accurately, the soul leaves the flesh or mortal aspect of our nature.) Our empirical experience in and with the communion of saints tells us that those who die in Christ continue to exist—to live—in him. Their state of existence can be properly termed ensouled. Certainly they have been subjected to the destructive power of death, just as Jesus was at his death on the cross. In Philippians 1.21–23, however, the apostle Paul alludes to an aspect of human existence—a critical stage on life's way—that can be termed an intermediate state between earthly and resurrected existence. After physical death and before the general resurrection at the last day, there is a time (or, perhaps better, a mode of existence, since physical death takes us beyond the bounds of time and space) that is "with Christ," a condition that Paul declares is "much better" than life in the flesh, or earthly existence. In that condition, the soul has indeed been torn away from the body of flesh, being subjected to the power of death. Yet "with Christ," in the presence and infinitely greater power of Christ, the soul awaits the final resurrection, when the dead, in their full somatic reality and integrity, will be raised to new and eternal life. Then "we shall be changed," transformed from a nature that is perishable to one that is imperishable (1 Cor 15.52–53).

It is the continuing existence of the soul into God's eternity that perhaps explains the well-known phenomenon of resuscitated patients—persons who have been pronounced clinically dead yet who preserve a degree of awareness of their surroundings until they are resuscitated, until, as we again misleadingly say, their soul "returns to their body." (In fact, the soul reunites with the flesh to reconstitute the psychic or ensouled earthly body.) This further explains how the saints, who as ensouled beings have entered into God's eternity, can be known as living souls, even though they are disembodied (or more accurately disenfleshed) persons. Because their existence is ensouled, even if not fleshly, we can be in communion with them. With all the deceased, they await the transformation of their ensouled existence into a "spiritual body" at the general resurrection, a transformation that will overcome the destructive and divisive consequences of death. This, in essence, is what the apostle Paul describes in 1 Corinthians 15.44, where he affirms that the psychic body (*sōma psychikon*) will be transformed into a spiritual body (*sōma pneumatikon*).

The human being is created at a specific moment in time and in a specific space, yet he or she is destined for eternal life. The soul (*psychē*), together with the flesh (*sarx*) and spirit (*pneuma*), are all created to constitute the body (*sōma*).[1] At death, the flesh decays, since it is mortal. The soul, however, is not destroyed. It is not subject to corruption. To the contrary, the soul continues to exist, with the potential to enjoy communion with God. Yet the soul awaits final reintegration into a newly constituted spiritual body at the universal resurrection.

Accordingly, early Christian theologians utterly rejected the Greek understanding of the relation between soul and body expressed by the Platonic wordplay *sōma-sēma* (body-tomb). This implies that the immortal and preexistent soul is entombed in the body, so that salvation consists in liberation of the soul and its return to the realm of divine existence, while the body suffers annihilation. Christianity, on the other hand, teaches resurrection of the body not as a complement to immortality of the soul but as its corrective. Resurrection of the body depends on Christ's victory over death, and hence the theological importance of the paschal hymn: "By his death he has trampled down death!" If the soul were in fact immortal, there would have been no need for that victorious death. It would suffice simply for us to die and thereby allow the soul to continue existing, unencumbered by the body. If the soul, however, is the animating principle that determines bodily integrity and personal identity, then physical death leads not to the soul's liberation but to its—again, tragic—separation from the flesh, thereby destroying the person's somatic

---

[1]Again we need to recall that St Paul never intended to present a systematic description of the body's constituent parts. Consequently, it is often difficult to tell when the term spirit refers to an aspect of human existence, when it is used synonymously with soul, or when it refers to the Spirit of God.

identity. That identity can be restored only through the death on the cross of the one who fully assumed our human nature, died in that nature, then rose and ascended, bearing that redeemed and restored nature in himself. Thereby, and only thereby, we can share in his death, resurrection, and glorification.

The two perspectives, immortality of the soul and resurrection of the body, are therefore essentially irreconcilable. And this, of course, raises questions about our Orthodox prayers that suggest that the two can in fact be reconciled. The problem would be resolved if, with St Irenaeus and patristic tradition in general, we substituted the term flesh for body, or prayed for the peaceful separation of the soul from the body of flesh. By this latter expression, we would be making the same distinction St Paul makes when he distinguishes the physical from the spiritual body. "Body of flesh" would refer to the mode of earthly existence that ends with physical death. The soul that separates from that body continues to "be with Christ" (Phil 1.23). Yet it awaits the transformation of the disintegrated person from an earthly to a heavenly body, from a psychic to a spiritual body, that will occur at the general resurrection. Then the soul will be fully integrated into the spiritual body, which in turn will fully restore personal integrity and identity.

The important point is that continuity from one state to another, from the physical to the spiritual body, is preserved by the somatic or bodily aspect of our being. A person's unique reality "is sown a physical body." Then that body dies and undergoes dissolution, because at death the soul departs, and this is followed by corruption of the flesh. The person's death is real and total, as was Christ's. But just as Christ rose from the dead in his resurrected and glorified body—yet retained full personal identity with the earthly condition that was his prior to his crucifixion—so we ourselves shall finally be raised up, not as a new and different person but as a renewed and transformed body. Our body will be changed from a physical to a spiritual body, from a body of death to a body of glory. But our personal identity will be preserved. What preserves that personal identity from earthly life, through death, and into resurrected existence is precisely the somatic continuity between earthly and heavenly existence, between the physical body and the spiritual body.

In 1 Thessalonians 5.23, St Paul employs a traditional tripartite formula: "may your spirit and soul and body be kept sound and blameless at the coming of our Lord Jesus Christ." This is unique in his writings. Normally he retains a Jewish perspective on the nature and elements of the human person, making a distinction between *sarx* and *pneuma*. To his mind, the real dualism that characterizes human existence is between flesh and spirit rather than between body and soul. *Sarx* (flesh), like the Hebrew *basar*, is not sinful as such; it represents the superficial aspect of our lives, subject to temptations, sickness, and death. The term flesh thus designates the fallen human condition, marked by passions and mortality. Spirit, on the other hand, designates the aspect of our being that is in communion with divine life, and as we have noted, it does so to the point that it is often difficult to determine whether Paul is speaking of the human spirit or the Spirit of God dwelling and acting within us (cf. 1 Cor 2.10–16).

Nevertheless, it is important to recognize a further distinction in St Paul's thought. The deeper sense of flesh and spirit in his anthropology refers not to two dimensions or elements of the human being but rather to two opposing orientations. One's entire being is oriented either toward the flesh, with its passions, mortal weakness, and tendency to rebel against the divine will, or it is oriented toward the spirit, which means it voluntarily submits itself to the authority and dominion of the Spirit of God (cf. Gal 5.16–25).

It would require a detailed exegesis to prove the point, but the body in Paul's perspective refers essentially to what we term the person (cf., for example, the use of the term body in passages such as 1 Cor 6.15–20; 7.4; and Eph 5.28; here *sōma* indicates the person as a whole; similarly, Mk 5.29 and parallels). Body in this sense signifies the entire composition of the created human being, including flesh, soul, mind, and spirit. Paul's anthropology, like that of the Jewish tradition in which he was raised, is holistic rather than dualistic. When he speaks of the body, he is normally referring to the whole person, created in the image of God and called to grow in Christ "from glory to glory" (2 Cor 3.18).

The Body of Glory

The phrase "body of glory" (*sōma tēs doxēs*) does not appear as such in the New Testament. The closest expression to it is *sōma tēs doxēs autou*, the "body of his glory," referring to the glorified body of the risen Lord (Phil 3.21). Yet the New Testament speaks frequently and eloquently about the glorification of the human person. We already mentioned Philippians 1.23, noting that it presupposes an intermediate stage of existence, between physical death and the general resurrection, during which the deceased believer is in immediate communion with Christ. We have noted as well 1 Corinthians 15.44 and its context and must return briefly to that passage. Finally, we need to consider 2 Corinthians 5.1–10, where the apostle speaks not of a transformation from one body to another but of our longing to "put on our heavenly dwelling."

There seems to be a progression in Paul's thought from 1 Corinthians to 2 Corinthians, and on to the final stage represented by the later letter to the Philippians. On the one hand, he never abandons the conviction, expressed in 1 Corinthians 15 concerning the universal resurrection, that God will transform our ensouled physical bodies (*sōma psychikon*) into glorified spiritual bodies. There is total somatic—that is, personal—continuity between the two. The physical body, bound by time and space, dies and is buried in the earth; it is raised up to share in Christ's own transcendent, glorified existence. The continuity between the two states, however, must be described precisely as somatic, and not material. Body, once again, refers to personal existence, created in the image of God and bearing that image into eternity.[2]

Paul's statements would raise fewer questions for us if he had referred to the form of our earthly existence as a *sōma sarkikon*, a "body of flesh." The fact that he speaks specifically of a psychic

---

[2]The question as to just when that transformation from the physical to the spiritual body will take place has troubled interpreters of every age. We are accustomed to envisioning the Parousia as occurring at the end of history, presumably in a far distant future. Since physical death leads to a form of existence that is beyond time and space, however, and since to the mind of God there is no duration but everything is immediately present, some interpreters hold that this transformation, together with judgment itself, occurs immediately after our physical death. (Is this what Paul is thinking in Phil 1.23?)

body apparently reflects his concern to combat certain gnosticizing tendencies in Corinth that would radically separate body and soul even in its earthly state, reflecting once again a Platonic dualism. The earthly body, for Paul, is the unified reality of flesh, mind, and spirit, governed by the soul, or divinely bestowed life principle. In the resurrection, the soul will be transformed with every other element of somatic existence to become a spiritual body, a body charged with the grace, the power, and the life of the Holy Spirit. The fallen image of earthly humanity will itself be transformed and restored to the original perfection in which and for which it was created (cf. Gen 1.26f). Thus Paul can declare, "Just as we have borne the image of the man of dust, we shall also bear the image of the man of heaven [Christ]" (1 Cor 15.49).

The fact that Paul was repeatedly persecuted and imprisoned may well have influenced the development in his thought between his first and second canonical letters to the Corinthians.[3] By the time he wrote the latter, he was aware that he would likely die before the Parousia, the second coming of Christ in glory. This led him to reflect on the state of the human person—the body or somatic existence—in the period between physical death and final resurrection.

In 2 Corinthians 5, therefore, he attempts to deal with this question in a way that contradicts his opponents (probably Hellenistic Jewish Christians) who held that death means the separation of the soul from the body, such that any intermediate existence would be necessarily bodiless, characterized by somatic "nakedness." Accordingly, he uses mixed images to declare that at death

[3]We know from 1 Cor 5.9 that the apostle wrote at least one letter to the Christians in Corinth that was not included in the Church's canon of Scripture.

we are not stripped of our somatic reality but rather we "put on a heavenly dwelling": "While we are still in this tent, we sigh anxiously; not that we would be unclothed, but that we would be further clothed, so that what is mortal may be swallowed up by life" (2 Cor 5.4).

The phrase "further clothed" renders the sense of the Greek verb *ependuomai*. The prefix *epi* could indeed signify putting one thing—a dwelling or a garment—over another. Yet the verb could also express a qualitative change, from the lowly earthly habitation to the glorious heavenly habitation, from a "garment of skin" (cf. Gen 3.21) characterized by weakness, passion, and mortality to a transfigured body that allows us to be "at home with the Lord" (2 Cor 5.8).[4]

A consistent theme appears in patristic commentaries on this passage in 2 Corinthians 5. It is the conviction that personal, somatic identity exists between the earthly body and the heavenly body. Origen declares, "In regard to our bodily nature we must understand that there is not one body which we now use in lowliness and corruption and weakness and a different one which we are to use hereafter in incorruption and power and glory, but that this same body, having cast off the weaknesses of its present existence,

---

[4]For a thoughtful discussion of the "garments of skin" and Orthodox anthropology in general, see Panayiotis Nellas, *Deification in Christ: The Nature of the Human Person* (Crestwood, NY: St Vladimir's Seminary Press, 1987). The flexibility and lack of systematic precision in Paul's language is well illustrated by the passage 2 Cor 5.6–10. Here body signifies our earthly existence as contrasted with the eternal "building from God" that awaits those who die in Christ. As the overall context of 2 Cor 5 indicates, however, that building, "eternal in the heavens," is the same as the "spiritual body" of 1 Cor 15.

will be transformed into a thing of glory and made spiritual."[5] Theodoret of Cyrrhus in Syria († ca. 466) makes the same point: "The heavenly body is not some different one but the one we have now, which will be transformed."[6] Yet the continuity between the two states of the body, earthly and heavenly, is so total that St Paul can declare regarding the mystical experience described in 2 Corinthians 12:2 that he was unaware whether he was "in the body" or "out of the body" (referring to the body of flesh or body of death). Even in this present psychic body, the most intimate communion with Christ is possible, including experience of "the third heaven," where Paul received ineffable "visions and revelations of the Lord."

In a similar vein, he can exhort the Corinthians, tempted to sexual immorality, to glorify God in their somatic reality: "Do you not know that your body is a temple of the Holy Spirit within you, which you have from God? You are not your own; you were bought with a price. Therefore, glorify God in your body!" (1 Cor 6.19–20).

In St Paul's understanding, our true death does not occur with the end of physical existence. Mortality has been defeated by the redemptive work of Christ, opening before us the possibility for new life even in the present age. Our true death, we need to

[5]Origen of Alexandria *On First Principles* 3.6.6, in *Ancient Christian Commentary on Scripture* [hereafter *ACCS*], vol. 7 (Downers Grove, IL: Inter-Varsity, 1999), 239. This perception of the body's destiny, unlike the Origenist notion of eternal, preexistent souls, conforms fully to Orthodox anthropology.

[6]Theodoret of Cyrrhus *Commentary on the Second Epistle to the Corinthians* 313, in *ACCS*, vol. 7, 240.

remember, occurs at *baptism*, with the transformation of the "old man" into the new. By baptism, Paul declares, "you have put on the new nature, which is being renewed in knowledge after the image of its Creator" (Col 3.10; cf. Eph 2.15; 4.24). Similarly, Paul can declare in Romans 6.4, "We were buried with him by baptism into death, so that as Christ was raised from the dead by the glory of the Father, we too might walk in newness of life." This is a present reality that characterizes our life in the flesh. In the perspective of the Gospel of John as well, the life of the age to come is already present and accessible to us: "He who hears my word and believes him who sent me has eternal life; he does not come into judgment, but has passed from death to life" (Jn 5.24).

The "realized eschatology" of the New Testament obliges us to make a thoroughgoing reassessment of the way we usually understand the relation between life and death, as well as between the body of death and the resurrected spiritual body. God has created us and destined us for glory (Rom 9.23; Col 3.4). Yet because we have already died and been co-buried (*synetaphēmen*) with Christ, and have been raised with him to lead a new life (*kainotēti zoēs*), we can here and now glorify God and share in his transcendent glory, even in our mortal bodies (Rom 6.4; 1 Cor 6.20).

The earthly body (*sōma sarkikon* or *psychikon*) is called to participate in the glory of God by means of its transformation into a spiritual body (*sōma pneumatikon*). This transformation, however, begins in the present age. It is initiated by baptism into the death and resurrection of Christ (2 Cor 4.10; Col 2.12); it is perfected through ongoing faith in Christ and obedience to his commandments (Jn 5.24); and it is brought to its ultimate fulfillment after physical death, with the second coming of Christ and the universal resurrection.

We are faced, therefore, with another Pauline paradox. On the one hand, the transformation from a physical to a spiritual body will occur "in a moment, in the twinkling of an eye, at the last trumpet" (1 Cor 15.51–53), at the Parousia and the final judgment. Yet this transformation is already underway, by virtue of baptismal grace and our present union with Christ. To resolve this tension between present and future, between our earthly somatic reality and the transfigured life to come, we can speak most appropriately not of future and realized eschatology but of what Fr Georges Florovsky called "inaugurated eschatology." Through sacramental grace and the indwelling power of the Holy Spirit within our psychic bodies, we participate already in the glory of the life to come. Nevertheless, the fulfillment still lies ahead. In our present condition of sinfulness and mortality, "we await a Savior, the Lord Jesus Christ, who will change our lowly body to be like his glorious body" (Phil 3.20–21).

The Paschal Victory

Orthodox anthropology, together with its eschatology, is profoundly rooted in biblical tradition. Its vision of life and death depends on the witness of Holy Scripture, which itself is shaped by the experience of the apostolic authors. St Paul suffered imprisonment and knew he might well follow his Lord to martyrdom. Yet Paul also knew the joy and ineffable wonder of a mystical vision so powerful that he was unable to determine whether he was in or outside of the body. His experience in the face of death and his unshakable hope in the promise of coming glory, the transformation of his physical body into a glorified spiritual body, can and should inform the approach every Christian takes to the mystery of death and the promise of eternal life.

In our tragically fallen world, it is tempting to dismiss the biblical promise of transfigured life as mere wishful thinking. For many people, the fact that life beyond death is void of proof leaves them void of hope. Yet the Church prays unremittingly for "a Christian ending to our lives," one in which the hope of resurrection and eternal life will be abundantly realized. A primary aspect of the Church's mission in the world, therefore, is to enable the faithful to live life and to face death with the hope of glory.

The most important conclusion we can draw from our overview of biblical themes can be stated in this way: For those who commit themselves to Christ, who submit themselves to his lordship, death is no longer an implacable enemy. Death in fact has been transformed into a paschal entryway into the kingdom of God. Our true death occurs at our baptism, when we die and are buried with Christ, in order to rise up with him in newness of life. From that moment onward, death has lost its sting. Because our mortal nature is marked by anxiety and doubt, we continue to struggle against our worst tendencies, against passions and temptations that threaten constantly to plunge us once more into an abyss of darkness and death. Yet even there, Christ is present. Even there we preserve the hope of glory. And that hope, as the apostle declares, "does not disappoint us, because God's love has been poured into our hearts through the Holy Spirit which has been given to us" (Rom 5.5).

That hope, unshakably established in the mind of the apostle, is shared equally by later representatives of the Orthodox spiritual tradition. It would be appropriate to close this chapter with a quotation attributed to one of those witnesses, St Macarius of Egypt, whose vision and language are thoroughly shaped by those of the apostle Paul:

> Every soul that through its own effort and faith is privileged in this present life to put on Christ completely, . . . and to unite with the heavenly light of [his] incorruptible image, is initiated here and now, personally, into the knowledge of all the heavenly mysteries. Moreover, in the great day of the resurrection, the body also will be glorified with that same heavenly image of glory. It will be caught up by the Spirit to the heavens, it will be given a form like the body of Christ's glory, and with him it will co-inherit the eternal kingdom.[7]

[7] St Symeon Metaphrastis, "Paraphrase of the Homilies of St Makarios of Egypt," in *The Philokalia*, vol. 3, eds. G. E. H. Palmer, Philip Sherrard, and Kallistos Ware (London: Faber and Faber, 1984), 348f (trans. slightly modified).

chapter seven

CARE IN THE FINAL STAGE OF LIFE

To care well for the dying, we must trust deeply that these people are loved as much as we are, and we must make that love visible by our presence. . . . We must encourage them to let go of their fears and to hope beyond the boundaries of death.
>   —Henri J. M. Nouwen, *Our Greatest Gift*

Death is better than a life of misery, and eternal rest than chronic sickness.
>   —Sirach 30.17

My desire is to depart and be with Christ, for that is far better.
>   —Philippians 1.23

Nearly twenty years ago, an aunt of mine committed suicide. She was the youngest in her generation and was always my favorite. We laughed and played together when I was a child, and when I proposed at the tender age of five, she promised with a broad smile that she would stop getting older and wait for me. I was delighted. Some four decades later, after her husband had died of cancer, she found herself caring for her oldest son, who had been seriously brain damaged in a tragic accident. Pressures accumulated, pushing her into a permanent state of depression. Although she was secure financially, she found her world crumbling away. I should have realized how deep her depression really was when she told me not to visit after I had planned a brief stopover at her home. ("I should have" . . . but I didn't.) I never saw her again.

The funeral was like so many others. People cried, her children tried to put on brave smiles, the pastor fumbled for something appropriate to say. As a young girl, my aunt had been turned away from the Church by a combination of verbal abuse and hypocrisy on the part of both clergy and lay members, people who should have known better. The pastor's eulogy was predictably banal, void of any real consolation or expression of hope. At the graveside, we gathered under a tent as he delivered another brief, empty prayer. The casket was set on the usual supports over the open grave. A green rug, supposed to imitate grass, had been thrown over the mound of dirt set to one side. Immediately after the prayer, to my astonishment, everyone turned to leave.

"My God," I blurted to no one in particular, "aren't we going to bury her?" "No," somebody replied. "The grave diggers take care of that." We left the cemetery, then family and a few close friends gathered in my aunt's living room for a little food. We spoke soothingly nice things to her children as we wandered around, taking in the transformation that had come about during the last months in her once beautiful home: her unmade bed, dishes all over the place, no pictures left on the walls, no curtains on the windows, empty wine bottles in the pantry. Finally, we left. All in all, it was a depressing and in some ways infuriating experience.

I couldn't help comparing that day with another my wife, Lyn, and I had shared with our boys, Paul and Michael, when they were about five and three respectively. We were living at the time in an old village house in a magnificent Swiss valley just north of Neuchâtel. Years before, the house had been divided into small apartments. Across the hall there lived three elderly women. One, Tante Jeanette, was suffering from Parkinson's disease. Each day toward the end of her life, our boys went into her room to play cards or just to sit by her bedside and tell her stories. Sometimes they took a spoon and carefully fed her, since she was no longer able to feed herself. They laughed with her, and when they came home, they cried a little, knowing they would soon lose her.

One winter evening, her sister appeared at the door to tell us that Jeanette had passed away. We hugged her, then the boys, and went across the hall. The sister opened the door to Jeanette's bedroom. Cold air washed over us as we stepped inside. The window was wide open, and several neighbors stood in corners of the room. There on the bed, propped up against pillows and surrounded by large clumps of lovely flowers, lay Jeanette, her eyes closed, looking more peaceful than we had ever seen her. Paul and Michael went over to her, touched her cold hand, and just stared. The look on their faces was one of sadness but also of wonder. They took it in with an understanding and acceptance that the adults in the room found hard to match. Finally, they both looked back at us and smiled.

The next day, the entire village gathered at the front of the house, some clutching flowers, others holding candles. A few men brought the casket down the narrow stairs and met the pastor at the village street. Then, while some sang quietly and others wept, we processed informally through the village, first to the church, then to the cemetery. With simple prayers and a eulogy spoken from the heart, the pastor, with the rest of us, laid Jeanette to rest.

Another story: When a dear older friend, Michael, was dying, he remained at home, where his family cared for him with extraordinary attention and affection. One morning, Lyn and I were called to the house by his devoted wife, who somehow had transferred Michael from the bed to an easy chair. When we entered the room, his eyes were closed. Several of us spoke to him, but there was no response. Finally, Lyn stood close to him, leaned down, and spoke loudly into his ear, "Good morning, Michael!" His eyes opened wide, then with a radiant, beatific smile, he looked at his wife and at the others in the room. A moment or two later, he closed his eyes again, and we left. Later that day, Michael died.

The burial was held in an old Russian cemetery some miles from the family home. As the celebrating priest, I offered the final prayers, then we sang the funeral hymn, and I stepped back. In Russian practice, family members and friends come forward at that moment, scoop up a handful of earth from an outstretched shovel, and drop it into the grave. After everyone had had their turn, Michael's family took up shovels to complete the burial by hand. Lyn took up a shovel too, and others joined in by turn. Shovelfuls of soil dropped with a hollow thump on the exposed casket, then it was soil on soil until there was a small mound over the grave. Each of us, working together, participated in that burial, acknowledging the tragedy and sadness of death, yet sharing through our tears the unshakeable conviction that Christ has destroyed the power of death and that Michael now reposes in all the fullness and joy of the communion of saints.

These vignettes have taught me a great deal about death, and perhaps still more about the way we are to care for dying persons. As my aunt was sinking ever farther into chronic depression, complicated by alcoholism, she isolated herself from both family and friends. Out of some distorted sense of discretion, afraid to interfere, we in effect abandoned her. Unable to care for her son as she felt she should, she became panicked, confused, and hopeless. Finally, she numbed herself with alcohol, got into her car, and started the engine in a closed garage. I could have cared more. I should have cared more. God knows how I wish I had cared more. But I didn't.

Nothing really redeems an act of abandonment, especially when we abandon those who are dying. Nevertheless, in his mercy God lets light shine out of the darkness, often in unexpected ways. It took our children, little kids with all their simple and heartfelt kindness, to teach me about the need to offer tenderness, affection, and personal warmth to those whose lives are slipping away. So too our joint participation in Michael's burial enabled us to share fully in the true significance of a dear friend's death: "Thine own of Thine own, we offer unto Thee."

How are we to care for dying people, and how are we to deal with the grief that follows their death? In this final chapter, I'd like to reflect a little on both of these questions. I would hope that something here might be of use to readers who find themselves confronted with the mystery of death, with all of its dread and hopefulness, its challenges and obligations. These remarks are, in some sense, complementary to my discussion of end-of-life care in an earlier book, *The Sacred Gift of Life*.[1] There I tried to deal with technical matters concerning appropriate measures to sustain life in terminally ill patients, together with ways to help those patients make their final paschal journey in peace and with dignity. My concern throughout was to provide a response to persons who defend practices the Church has always rejected and must continue to reject, including euthanasia and physician-assisted suicide. I also dealt to some degree with matters of terminal life-support, together with questions raised by so-called hard cases, in which decisions have to be made, on a case-by-case basis, to bring relief to suffering persons in a way that conforms to the will of God as we know it from Scripture and the Church's tradition.

Here I would like to return to some of those issues in a less formal and more personal way. The thread that connects these reflections, at least in my mind, is that of care. In more biblical language, the question is how we can offer to dying patients a depth and quality of love that will most effectively guide them along the final stages of the pathway that leads from this earthly existence to life in the kingdom of God.

[1]Breck, *The Sacred Gift of Life*. See chap. 5, "A Blessed Pascha: Approaching the End of Life," and esp. 223-39.

First of all, it is essential that we recognize the utter distortion that the "American way of death" imposes on believing Christians as well as on others. We have become so accustomed to a "Forest Lawn approach" to death and burial—in which death is sanitized or simply hidden—that we have lost any real sensibility toward the mystery that properly surrounds the end stage of life and the transition to life beyond. In his widely read book *The Denial of Death*, Ernest Becker explains the nearly universal denial of the phenomenon itself as due to the "terror" associated with death.[2] For many Christians, this is terror of the unknown, coupled with fear that God's judgment will outweigh his mercy to the point that if indeed there is an afterlife, they may well spend it in hell, a place of separation from God where they will be subjected to eternal punishment. Given what many Christian children are taught about heaven and hell at home and in Sunday school, it's no wonder that many of them grow up hoping that death means simply annihilation, yet dreading the possibility that it will lead to vengeful retribution for their sins. And it's no wonder that so many, at least in this country, cling to the fundamentalist and wholly unbiblical hope of "once saved, always saved," in which the "once" depends on nothing more demanding than standing up in church one day and "taking Jesus as my personal Lord and Savior." This expediency has for many people attenuated, at least somewhat, the terror of death. It has done little, however, to enable them to face death realistically, much less to embrace it as a passageway to a glory and joy beyond all comprehension.

If Orthodoxy is less certain about salvation than the fundamentalists are, it is far more realistic about the narrow path that leads

[2]Ernest Becker, *The Denial of Death* (New York: Free Press, 1973).

to it. If Orthodox Christians expect that pathway to be long and arduous, filled with stumbling blocks that need constantly to be removed through repentance, fasting, confession, and ascetic discipline, they also know that the love of God is stronger than death and that the mercy of God will enable them in the end to share fully and eternally in Christ's victory over death.

To an Orthodox believer, the only sense, the only meaning, to be found in death, is given by what lies beyond. This includes judgment and ongoing purification. It is a process that never ends, yet it is one that culminates in what Tradition calls *theōsis*, eternal participation in the very life of God himself. This is what the young man had in mind when he answered the question, Why did you become Orthodox? "I became Orthodox," he replied, "in order to learn to die well." To die well is the deepest desire and the most realistic goal any of us can have. It can take a lifetime of effort, or by God's grace, it can be granted in the last moments of our biological existence. In either case, a "good death" is what we desire, what we most fervently long for, because a good death is the means by which we attain hereafter an everlasting, blessed, and joy-filled communion with the God of love.[3]

Most of our contemporaries dismiss this kind of talk as "pie in the sky bye and bye." It's a convenient illusion we have created in order to deal with the terror of death and the distress that so often leads us there. The multitudes of near-death experiences—with a

---

[3]Stanley Harakas summarizes this point as follows: "The only 'good death' for the Orthodox Christian is the peaceful acceptance of the end of his or her earthly life with faith and trust in God and the promise of the Resurrection" (Stanley Harakas, *Contemporary Moral Issues* [Minneapolis: Light and Life, 1982], 176).

---

tunnel opening out onto beautiful vistas filled with brilliant light, and the welcoming appearance of deceased loved ones—are dismissed as the product of brain chemistry, a purely neurological reaction to the snuffing out of life. This leaves us with little more than Dylan Thomas's refusal to "go gentle into that good night" and his cry to "rage, rage against the dying of the light!"

The Church has never said anything definitive about near-death experiences, and rightly so. They are, after all, near death and not death itself. So how do we know?

What we do know, however, is what has been handed down since Jesus' own death and the death of the earliest Christian martyrs. It is the truth that death is not an end but a beginning. The end of our biological life is not an end at all but the marking of a rebirth, one that began with our baptism and comes to fulfillment in the eternal communion of saints. As the apostle Paul declares in Romans 6.4, our real death occurs when we die and are buried with Christ in the baptismal waters of regeneration. It is from there that we rise up "in newness of life" to embark on a journey, an adventure of mind, body, and soul, that will lead, like Christ's own journey, through suffering and death and into paradise. To some, this may be pie in the sky. To untold millions of believers, including countless martyrs who gave up their lives willingly, even gladly, it is reality itself. It is a reality revealed by the biblical witness, attested to by the saints—whose knowledge of such things vastly surpasses our own—and confirmed in the life of each of us by the prayer we offer up constantly, both personally and within the liturgical community, for those who have preceded us into the place that only weak and inadequate poetic images can describe: a place of brightness, a place of refreshment, a place of repose, where all sickness, sorrow, and sighing have passed away.

This is the faith of the Church and perhaps the Christian's most fervent hope. When I'm at peace with myself and the world around me, it's my belief and my hope as well. At other times, I have to admit, I can find myself in a suffocating black fog of doubt. Occasionally in those times, I find myself, too, staring at the face of Christ depicted in an icon, and begging with tears, "Please, please, let it be true!" Consolation comes with the realization that the doubt I often experience is invariably linked with a depressing level of fatigue, discouragement, anger, or frustration. Light begets light. When the light is there, by some miracle, the devil takes his leave, and faith—the fragile but sure conviction that indeed it is true—is restored.

Euthanasia: A Good Death?

The question remains as to how we can best care for and accompany those who are preparing, knowingly or unknowingly, to make that final journey. Before we speak of specific forms of care, though, it is necessary to address an issue that takes up as much space in today's newspapers as it does in the latest ethics journals. This is the issue of euthanasia, not only its definition but also its application in countries that have ventured a little farther than we have down the proverbial slippery slope.

The term euthanasia, as we know, originally signified a "good death" (*ev-thanasia*). Today, in the minds of most Orthodox and many other Christians, it signifies an action just short of murder. This is because the expression is now used to designate direct, active intervention, usually on the part of a physician, whose purpose is to hasten death in what are purportedly the interests of a critically ill or dying patient.[4] Because we are accustomed (and quite rightly so) to basing our moral choices on Scripture, beginning with the Ten Commandments, we instinctively recoil from an action of this kind, taking it to be a direct violation of the order not to kill.

Our opposition to procedures that hasten death is only intensified by what we are presently observing in England, Belgium, and the Netherlands, where euthanasia has become publicly accepted policy. As long as they follow certain guidelines, physicians in those countries may practice euthanasia without fear of prosecution. This strikes most of us as a wanton abandonment of traditional values in health care, whose primary aim for more than two millennia has been the Hippocratic concern to "do no harm," to cure rather than to kill. The entire picture has been made all the more bleak by recent revelations that Dutch physicians have been routinely practicing euthanasia on newborn infants whose quality of life is so compromised by disease or deformity that, to the doctors' eyes, it seems hardly worth living.

Here certain absolutes definitely have their place. Orthodox Christianity cannot be anything but pro-life when it comes to

---

[4]The Roman Catholic "Declaration on Euthanasia," issued by the Congregation for the Doctrine of the Faith on May 5, 1980, defines euthanasia as follows: "By euthanasia is understood an action or an omission which of itself or by intention causes death, in order that all suffering may in this way be eliminated. Euthanasia's terms of reference, therefore, are to be found in the intention of the will and in the methods used." (Text reproduced in the *National Catholic Bioethics Quarterly* 1, no. 3 [2001]: 433.)

matters of abortion, and the same holds for euthanasia. The Church recognizes that a fundamental difference exists between "killing" and "letting die," between deliberately taking a life and allowing a patient to succumb to disease or trauma without being subjected to medical heroics.

In the experience of some patients and their physicians, however, there comes a point where unavoidable choices in health-care strategies lead perilously close to what is called "mercy killing." It is easy for us to reject the very idea of such a solution. We may believe that pain management and overall palliative care can prove sufficient to ease every dying patient through the last days and hours of earthly life. Any medical professional who has dealt intensively with terminal patients, though, knows full well that these measures are not always successful. And therein lies a dilemma that we need to recognize and take seriously, both medically and morally. Where does this lead us in today's debate over euthanasia?

"Hard cases make bad law," they teach in law school, and the same holds true in the field of medicine. Yet hard cases exist, cases in which pain and associated distress cannot be adequately controlled, with the result that the patient is pressed to despair. Some Orthodox Christians affirm that we should not try to palliate the suffering of those who are wasting away with debilitating illnesses or other infirmities, since it allows them to "share in the sufferings of Christ." That's easy to say when it's someone else or someone else's loved one who is going through the agony. Certain degrees of suffering can indeed be redemptive, as many saints attest. Nevertheless, no one can fully appreciate the depth of suffering borne by another person. Some patients are afflicted with a level of intractable physical pain and consequent psychological and spiritual anguish that for most of us is unimaginable and would be unbearable. They may have intestinal tumors that cause them to vomit their own fecal matter, or their lives may be consumed by a desperate and unrelieved struggle simply to breathe. To declare on principle that they should bear their anguish as though it were God's will that they suffer is irresponsible and theologically obtuse. Christ, the eternal Son of God, has borne the world's suffering, and by it he has destroyed the power of death and corruption. Some people may have a specific vocation to drink the cup of their physical agony to the bitter dregs. Most of us, however, do not. Therefore we need to avoid glib pronouncements about the value of suffering, not to deny that value but to set it in its proper perspective and acknowledge its proper limits.

The subject of euthanasia, then, arises especially in a limited but significant number of cases in which terminally ill patients are experiencing a level of pain and distress they can no longer cope with. There is a time to live and a time to die, and both need to be respected. Yet this raises the question as to just how, from a Christian moral perspective, the dying person may be appropriately accompanied and assisted through that terminal phase.

Medical technology has made prodigious advancements in recent years. Ventilators, dialysis machines, MRIs, and antibiotics, for example, have improved and extended the lives of vast numbers of grateful patients. In many cases, however, that same technology has merely prolonged the dying process, and there it is counterproductive. A surgically implanted pacemaker can significantly extend the life and functioning of a cardiac patient. Cardiopulmonary resuscitation (CPR) practiced on an elderly person who has suffered a major heart attack, on the other hand, often does little more than produce cracked ribs or restore an oxygen-deprived brain to a level of existence that is merely vegetative. (CPR has produced an important caveat that extends the string of acronyms: "If you've opted for DNR, don't call EMS!")[5] Pneumonia in a dying patient can easily be cured today by antibiotics. That cure, however, means that the patient must finally succumb to some other pathology, often more distressful and more painful. A ventilator can be lifesaving in cases where a lung has collapsed or a curable disease is attacking a person's respiratory system. But used on a patient dying of ALS (amyotrophic lateral sclerosis, or Lou Gehrig's disease), it merely increases the anguish of slow suffocation and prevents what Orthodox Christians pray for every day: a painless and peaceful end to their earthly existence.

General recognition of the quandary we often find ourselves in thanks to the very real marvels of modern medical technology has led the public, as well as medical professionals, to an important conclusion regarding end-of-life care. In terminal cases (in which the length of survival is measured in terms of days or hours), it is appropriate to withhold or withdraw life support and to allow the dying process to complete its course. Often referred to as "passive euthanasia," this procedure in fact conforms thoroughly both to the Hippocratic Oath and to the will of God as we know

---

[5]DNR: a "do not resuscitate" order, often inscribed on the chart of a hospitalized, terminally ill patient (and too often ignored by the medical team). EMS: the emergency medical service, which in most cases (unless the person is carrying an officially sanctioned DNR order) is legally obligated to perform CPR on live but nonbreathing victims of stroke, heart attack, or other traumas, even when they have been deprived of oxygen for many minutes and have suffered severe and irreversible damage to the brain.

it from Scripture and the tradition of the Church. It respects the patient's need to find relief from his or her suffering, it acknowledges the limits of technology in achieving cures, and it allows the patient to complete his earthly journey with as much peace and dignity as possible. When medical intervention in terminal cases neither palliates nor cures but merely draws out the dying process, it becomes unacceptably burdensome and should be discontinued. In such situations, passive euthanasia (as regrettable and misleading as that expression happens to be) is morally acceptable, even obligatory.[6]

But what of "voluntary active euthanasia"? VAE implies the willingness on the part of a terminally ill patient to accept direct intervention by the physician, with the specific aim of hastening death. With VAE, both the patient and the doctor intend to bring on the patient's death more quickly than it would occur naturally if the disease or trauma were left to run its course.

Here, as happens so often, we as a society have become thoroughly polarized on a critical issue. Pro-life voices raise the claim that no such active intervention is morally permissible, including

---

[6]The Roman Catholic "Declaration on Euthanasia" expresses this point in its series of "clarifications": "When inevitable death is imminent in spite of the means used, it is permitted in conscience to take the decision to refuse forms of treatment that would only secure a precarious and burdensome prolongation of life, so long as the normal care due to the sick person in similar cases is not interrupted. In such circumstances the doctor has no reason to reproach himself with failing to help the person in danger." A similar position is taken by Orthodox ethicists. See especially Harakas, *Contemporary Moral Issues*, 166–76; and N. Hatzinikolaou, "Prolonging Life or Hindering Death? An Orthodox Perspective on Death, Dying and Euthanasia," *Christian Bioethics* 9, nos. 2–3 (2003): 187–201.

physician-assisted suicide, where the doctor prescribes or otherwise makes available to a patient medication that the patient self-administers in order to bring on death. Right-to-die advocates, on the other hand, make absolute claims to individual autonomy, insisting that we have the right to end our lives when and as we please. As with the abortion debate, the issue of euthanasia has led to a nuance-free "dialogue of the deaf."

In trying to find a suitable approach to the most vexing questions surrounding terminal care, people who deal with dying patients often have recourse to the "principle of double effect." This principle attempts to guide ethical decision-making in situations where an action deemed necessary will inevitably, yet foreseeably, result in some wrong or evil as a secondary consequence. For example, a mastectomy will inevitably leave massive scar tissue, yet despite this unwanted and yet foreseen consequence, a malignant lump in the breast clearly justifies the decision to operate. In the case at hand, the principle of double effect would be applied to help discern what actions may be morally taken to relieve the suffering of a dying patient and to help that patient reach the end of his or her life in peace. The principle is usually expressed in terms of four conditions:

1. The action itself, independent of its effects or consequences, must be inherently good or at least morally neutral.

2. The evil effect must not be the means for producing the desired effect.

3. That evil, even if foreseeable, must not be intended.

4. The action that produces the evil effect must be proportionate, both to the need addressed by that action and to the evil that results from it. (We should not shoot a pesky fly with a shotgun or guillotine someone to cure a headache.)

The principle of double effect recognizes that actions often produce results that are both good and evil. It is applied in an effort to determine what action may be performed, and under what conditions, when the good effect expected of the action will be unavoidably accompanied by some evil consequence. The principle is useful insofar as it provides a framework for dealing with ambiguous moral choices. It often falters, however, when we consider the third condition: that the evil action may be foreseen but must not be intended.

In cases of terminal illness, it is unreasonable and unrealistic to expect that a physician, acting in good conscience and in the best interests of the patient, will not also desire that the patient's suffering end in death, sooner rather than later. That desire will inevitably affect the doctor's intention. For example, in patients who are in the end stage of life and who are enduring excruciating, intractable pain, the physician will normally opt to increase the dosage of morphine or other opiates in order to relieve the patient's suffering as much as possible. Yet beyond a certain level, morphine can repress the respiratory system and hasten death.[7]

[7]This has recently been called into question, however. John F. Peppin, "Palliative Sedation at the End of Life," *Christian Bioethics* 9, nos. 2–3 (August–December 2003): 343–55, cites studies that demonstrate the contrary: "High or low dose or rate of change in the opiate dose has been found to have no effect on survival of terminal patients" (348). The same is true

The physician and the patient thus find themselves in a dilemma. Even if they are both philosophically opposed to euthanasia, they may deeply desire that the suffering end in the only way possible: by the patient's death. It is unreasonable to expect that the doctor will be able to suppress that desire as he augments the dosage of opiates, simply to avoid in his own mind—or that of the patient or the patient's proxy—the idea that he is intentionally performing an act that will bring on death more quickly than if the action were not performed and the patient were allowed (obliged) to suffer until the bitter end.

A proposed solution to this dilemma has recently received a great deal of publicity. It is the matter of "palliative sedation" (PS; also called "terminal sedation").[8] In those cases in which pain management is inadequate to alleviate the patient's agony, it is possible to induce a state of semiconsciousness or unconsciousness in which pain is minimally perceived or no longer experienced.

The French Society for the Accompaniment of the Dying and Palliative Care[9] has published studies on PS that clearly define

with the use of opioids. (This entire issue of *Christian Bioethics* is devoted to euthanasia and physician-assisted suicide and contains many informative articles from a variety of Christian perspectives.)

[8]Palliative care, of which PS is one aspect, is directed toward persons in the terminal phase of life, with the intent to alleviate pain and other symptoms, both physical and psychological, through appropriate medication and other therapy. It should seek a balance between decreasing pain while preserving consciousness. It can involve the use of radiation and chemotherapy, whose aim in terminal cases is less to heal than to relieve suffering. To my mind, it should include as well appropriately supervised and administered uses of medical marijuana, where no other therapies prove effective.

[9]*Société Française d'Accompagnement et de Soins Palliatifs* (SFAP).

ethical modalities of the practice. Its members are fully aware of the danger of "clandestine euthanasia," as they are of the need to administer sedatives only to the degree necessary to relieve acute suffering—and then only in patients who are at the end stage of life. This means that the condition of each patient must be considered to be unique, demanding case-specific treatment. The medical team begins by determining whether the patient is actually in a terminal phase because of the irreversible breakdown of some vital respiratory, cardiovascular, or neurological function. In cases of acute distress (a catchall term for various forms of unrelenting pain and suffering), sedation may be called for in order to lessen to the degree necessary a level of physical and psychological agony the patient finds intolerable. This can mean inducing a state of light sleep from which the patient can be awakened by a voice or simple stimulus. In more difficult cases, it can mean inducing a coma, either transitory or prolonged until the patient dies. The caregivers resort to this latter protocol, however, only when every other available method to assuage unbearable pain and suffering has been tried and found wanting. And of course, it is permissible only in cases in which the patient or the patient's proxy has given informed consent.[10]

[10]Midazolam is the recommended sedative used in terminal cases (in which death is imminent), because it meets the basic criteria of ease of use and reversibility, short half-life (two to four hours), dose-dependent sedative effect, and solubility in water that allows for various means of administration. See the report of the SFAP, *"Première journée d'actualités médicales en soins palliatifs,"* (held on October 11, 2002 at the Pfizer Laboratories, 23–25 avenue du Docteur Lannelongue, 75668 Paris cedex 14), including the report by Veronique Blanchet, M.D., *"Situations extrêmes, symptomes incontrolables et place de la sédation,"* 217–22. She includes in her bibliography N. Cherny and R. K. Portenoy, "Sedation in the Management of Refractory Symptoms: Guidelines for Evaluation and Treatment," *Journal of Palliative Care* (1994): 10:31–39.

When it is properly administered, PS does not hasten the patient's death, at least not appreciably. And the often-expressed fear that the patient may still experience pain even under sedation seems unfounded, given the evidence to the contrary provided by MRIs, PET scans, and other data.[11] Some objections to PS have been raised because the usual practice, once the patient is sedated, is to withdraw or withhold food and fluids. Concerns that the patient will die of hunger or thirst, however, are also unfounded. The average patient placed under palliative sedation dies not from the sedation itself but from the underlying pathology, within two to four days. As long as mucous membranes in the patient's body are properly hydrated, effects of withholding food and liquid are negligible.

However effective PS may be in addressing problems of severe pain and distress in terminal patients, it is clear that every attempt must first be made to provide adequate pain management short of sedation. Different patients perceive pain differently. For many, it is complicated and intensified by psychological stress or depression. In such cases, relief may well be provided by common tranquilizers or mild sedatives that allow the patient to remain conscious. This is of particular importance for Christian patients, in that it allows them to complete critical end-of-life tasks such as personal sharing with loved ones, seeking forgiveness, making a final confession, and receiving the Holy Eucharist.

The point we need to recognize is that these cases of acute, unrelieved pain are largely responsible for the increase in patients' demands for physician-assisted suicide and euthanasia.

[11]Peppin, "Palliative Sedation," 344–45.

Although improvements have been made in recent years, our medical schools are notorious for their failure to prepare their students in the crucial matter of addressing pain, particularly in the terminally ill. This is a medical problem, but it is also a moral and spiritual problem of the greatest importance. When the veterinarian "put down" our dog recently, he watched as the injection took effect within seconds. He touched the dog's open eyes and stroked its sides, obviously moved by the loss of this very sick animal that he had cared for over the years. Then, with tears in his eyes, he said quietly, "I wish so much I could have done that for my suffering father." There are other ways, I wanted to tell him. Other ways, if only we have the wisdom, the courage, and the intelligence to develop them wisely and use them with compassion.

It is time for the Church, through its hierarchy, parish communities, and publications to address the issue of end-of-life care with a renewed focus and a genuine sense of urgency. It would seem appropriate for our Orthodox physicians, together with those of their colleagues who share their views, to take the following steps: (1) urge medical schools to include in their curricula an adequate number of courses on pain management and palliative care; (2) discuss among themselves and the general public, in all appropriate venues, the morality of practices such as terminal or palliative sedation, in an effort to reach a consensus that conforms to the mind of the Church; (3) militate peacefully yet forcefully against the immoral expediency of active voluntary euthanasia and physician-assisted suicide; and (4) in their parishes and other appropriate settings, engage in open and serious debate about the best way, both medically and spiritually, to accompany dying patients in the final stage of life, and particularly those who experience intolerable suffering and pain.[12]

Orthodox Christianity cannot accept the solution of active euthanasia, however popular that solution may be in any given society. We need to identify viable, morally acceptable alternatives by which physicians and the rest of us can accompany dying persons and assure them a peaceful and painless end to their lives. To determine those alternatives, however, requires an effort on the part of everyone concerned—and we are all concerned with illness and death. It requires that we seek, in mutual debate and in prayer, a discernment that ultimately only God can provide.

Care for the dying is a profoundly spiritual matter. It is one of the most important yet most neglected aspects of the Church's ministry. However we may decide with regard to specific protocols, the first task of that ministry, like the physician's primary responsibility, is to "do no harm." As many dedicated medical professionals have pointed out, it is not always possible to cure, yet it is always possible to care. It is that single-minded focus on compassionate care that will enable us most appropriately and most effectively to offer the life of the dying patient into God's loving and merciful safekeeping.

[12]Two articles provide excellent resources for this kind of shared reflection: Daniel B. Hinshaw and Jane Carnahan Hinshaw, "A Christian Ending to Our Life," *St Vladimir's Theological Quarterly* 44, no. 1 (2000): 61–82; and Daniel B. Hinshaw, "Spiritual Issues at the End of Life," *Clinics in Family Practice* 6, no 2 (June 2004): 423–40. The authors, both physicians, and members of an Orthodox parish in Michigan, have done extensive work in the area of palliative care. See as well the useful and informative collection of articles by Vigen Guroian, *Life's Living toward Dying: A Theological and Medical Ethical Study* (Grand Rapids, MI: Eerdmans, 1996).

Care for the Permanently Incapacitated

Just how is that compassionate care to be given to patients who are not terminally ill, yet because of sickness or severe trauma are permanently unresponsive to external stimuli and therefore are incapable of any conscious interaction with the world around them? This is a question we need to raise, particularly in light of recent highly publicized cases of patients who are trapped in a persistent or permanent vegetative state (PVS).[13]

PVS is a condition, often referred to as brain death, brought on by severe and irreversible damage to the cerebral hemispheres. It leaves the patient with no capacity for self-awareness or ability to relate to others. Since the brain stem is intact, however, autonomic and motor reflexes function normally. (The brain stem regulates basic body functions, including breathing, blood pressure, and heart rate. The left and right hemispheres make up the cerebrum and are covered by the cortex, the familiar gray layer of nerve cells that enable us to think, create, remember, communicate, and pray. Other portions of the brain, such as the cerebellum and the limbic system, handle more primitive functions, including the fight-or-flight response, balance, and sleeping. It is the cortex that makes possible our higher functions of thought and the capacity for personal relationships. If the cerebrum, including the cortex, is permanently destroyed, then we can say that personal identity is lost. While the soul is the life principle of

[13]Some clinicians refer to this condition during the first few months as persistent. Beyond that point, when recovery is deemed impossible, it is labeled permanent. Because of the connotations of "vegetative," there is a move on currently to change the designation to "post-coma unresponsiveness" (PCU).

the entire organism, death of the cerebrum indicates that the soul, in liturgical language, has "left the body"[14] and the person as such is dead.)

Because the brain stem and portions of the limbic system still function, PVS patients experience ordinary sleep-wake cycles and often emit sounds that can be misunderstood as attempts to speak. In fact, in such patients there is no cognition and no perception of stimuli, indicating that the cerebrum is no longer playing its vital role. Where this so-called vegetative state has persisted for more than a few months, there are no documented cases of recovery. (The term vegetative refers to the condition; it does not imply that the patient is less than human.) A person in PVS, then, is brain dead, even if a distinction can be drawn between their actual state and a condition of deep coma.[15]

Since prolonging the life of a PVS patient by means of life support affords no discernable benefit but merely imposes a continued burden, many medical professionals today argue that artificially administered nutrition and hydration may be withheld or withdrawn, providing the patient has given informed consent to the procedure through a living will or via a proxy with durable power of attorney. The much-publicized case of Terri Schiavo, however, illustrates just how important it is that a proper diagnosis be made when a patient is thought to be in a persistent or permanent vegetative state.

---

[14]As we pointed out in the preceding chapter, it would be more accurate to state that the soul separates from or has left the flesh.

[15]For a medical description of the condition, see *The Merck Manual*, 17th ed. (Rahway, NJ: Merck Sharp and Dohme Research Laboratories, 1999).

Schiavo was diagnosed as being in PVS, and after a great deal of legal wrangling, her husband succeeded in having her feeding tube removed. Nearly two weeks later, on March 31, 2005, she died of dehydration. Although the autopsy showed that her brain had been irreversibly damaged, Terri had nevertheless displayed clear signs of responsiveness to the presence of her family and priest, signs that were recorded on film. It seems, in other words, that she was not in a true vegetative state as that expression is properly defined. She was severely brain damaged but not brain dead.

If that in fact was the case, then Terri's death by forced dehydration was devoid of any moral justification. The matter would have been quite different if she had declared in a living will, prior to the events that left her disabled, just what kind of care she wanted if and when she became unable to make medical decisions. She could have stipulated, for example, that unless she were terminally ill or verifiably brain dead, she would want to be maintained on food and water. Or if a situation arose in which she was suffering from severe and chronic pain, she could have expressed the desire to be allowed to die, not by euthanasia but as a result of the underlying pathology. Absent such a will, the courts and her husband were able to euthanize her by mandating removal of her feeding tube.[16]

Since the early 1980s, it has been clinically established that withholding food and hydration from terminally ill patients—those who are actively engaged in the dying process—can be beneficial. It allows the buildup of nitrogen wastes that produce azotemia, a natural analgesic, and can enable the patient to slip into a coma

[16]See the article "Maggie, Terri and the Problem of Life-Support," in the Life in Christ series, www.oca.org, posted on July 1, 2005.

and die peacefully. On the other hand, continuing to provide food and water through intubation in terminal cases can increase the patient's sense of pain and suffering, without offering a proportionate benefit.[17]

Whatever Terri Schiavo's actual condition at the time of her death, the question raised by her case is whether it is ever morally and medically appropriate to remove food and hydration from a patient in PVS. Such patients are not, in the strict sense, terminally ill; they are not actually dying, even when there is no chance for recovery. Provided with food and water, they can live for months or even years. Yet their physical existence is preserved only by life-support technology and they remain in a state of permanent unconsciousness. If that technology were not available, such patients would quickly die, since they are incapable of feeding themselves or of being fed orally.

Catholic moral theologians have long debated whether providing nutrition and hydration to patients in PVS falls into the area of ordinary or extraordinary means. If the former, then such treatment is ethically mandatory; if the latter, then, weighing burdens against benefits, it may be morally appropriate to withdraw all life support and allow the patient to die. Pope John Paul II's declaration on the subject in March 2004 made it clear that he located the providing of food and water in the realm of ordinary means, and therefore it is morally obligatory in cases of PVS. Many Catholic ethicists, however, feel otherwise. They argue that there comes a point in a person's life when administering artificial

[17]See the discussion on "Nutrition and Hydration for the Terminally Ill" in Breck, *Sacred Gift of Life*, 234–39.

nutrition and hydration merely hinders the patient from attaining what we request in our Orthodox prayers: a "peaceful separation of soul and body," "a painless, blameless, and peaceful" end to earthly life and the passing on of the person to the ultimate end of human existence, which is eternal communion with God in the kingdom of heaven.

In light of those prayers and the Orthodox perspective on the mystery of death, we need to have as our primary concern the best interests of the patient. No one wants to lose a beloved friend or family member. Accordingly, we face a strong temptation (and often pressure) to do everything possible to ward off death, even if it means preserving a minimal level of existence by purely artificial means. We need to ask, though, whether such actions serve the interests and well being of the patient, or whether they derive from our own reluctance to accept the loss associated with death and to surrender the person into the hands of God.

This raises the question of the quality of the patient's life. Often the decision to provide or withhold nutrition and hydration is made on the basis of a subjective judgment as to whether the patient's existence is worth preserving. The issue has unfortunately been polarized between those who argue for "sanctity of life criteria" (life is inherently sacred, therefore it must be preserved at all costs) and those who argue for "quality considerations" (if that life is deemed worthless or pointless, then there is no obligation to preserve it).

This way of raising the question, however, is false and misleading. All human life is inherently sacred, and it is precisely that sacredness that invests it with its ultimate and indelible quality. This means again, however, that "there is a time to live and a time to die." Death in a paschal perspective is no longer "the last enemy." Death itself has been destroyed, and "we are given life." From the time of our conception until the end of our physical existence, the very purpose of our being is to allow the Holy Spirit to work within us the transformation from a body of death to life in Christ, a life that begins in the present age and endures through and beyond physical death into the fullness of life in the kingdom of God.

When a person is actually dying—when the soul is struggling to separate from the flesh—then, again, it may be morally permissible, even obligatory, to withhold nutrition and hydration in order that death may come naturally, as a regretted end but a blessed beginning to a new order of existence. Can we say the same of patients in PVS, who, technically, are not terminal?

All we can conclude, it seems, is this. Where it can be determined with certainty that brain death has occurred and there is no chance for recovery other than through God's own miraculous intervention (which can occur at any point), then it seems reasonable to conclude that artificial means of life support, including nutrition and hydration, may be morally withdrawn or withheld. In cases of PVS or deep coma, however, this procedure can be judged morally acceptable only to the degree that it can be definitively established that the condition is irreversible, that the cortex and hemispheres of the brain are indeed dead, and that the organism is functioning only because the brain stem is still intact.

Many medical professionals today would insist on "whole brain death" (including the brain stem) as the final criterion for determining whether the person is actually dead. It seems, nevertheless, that an adequate measure is "death of the brain as a whole" rather than "death of the whole brain." If the cerebrum has been irreversibly destroyed, then there is no possibility for any form of consciousness. The soul does not reside in the brain, to be sure. A brain-dead adult, though, is comparable to an anencephalic newborn. The body is without question fully human and worthy of respect. The most appropriate and compassionate treatment the medical team can offer an anencephalic child is to provide warmth and comfort (more for the sake of the parents than for the child, who is unable to perceive any positive or negative stimulus), and to allow the child to die from its condition. The same is true in cases where death of critical portions of the brain has occurred and there is no chance for improvement (other than by means of extraordinary divine intervention). In such cases, the person indeed is struggling to expire, to release the last breath from their body, to allow the soul to separate from the flesh, and artificial life support merely impedes that necessary process. This is a time not for medical solutions but for prayer. It is a time to acknowledge the limits of medical intervention, to celebrate the life that has crossed the threshold of death, and to surrender the person into the waiting arms of God.

The final judgment in all such cases needs to be made not by distinguishing ordinary from extraordinary means but by weighing the possibilities for cure. Where further medical intervention is futile and merely hinders the person in his or her struggle to die, then such intervention should be judged to be abusive rather than beneficial. Medical heroics in such a case are morally inappropriate.

Yet any decision to remove life support, particularly in nonterminal cases such as PVS, must be taken as the fruit of ardent and disinterested intercession on behalf of the patient. This does not mean that we should expect that an answer to the question regarding appropriate treatment or nontreatment will be written on the wall. It means that members of the church community— including the family, friends, and insofar as possible the medical team—offer the patient to God through ceaseless intercession, asking for both clarity and charity in making what could be their final decision regarding that patient's future and well being.

In the final analysis, everything depends on our motive. Where our primary concern is for the ultimate healing and salvation of the person in question, then we can make decisions, even in a state of uncertainty and confusion, with the confidence that God, in his time and in his way, will work for that person the paschal miracle that leads from a dying life through physical death, and into life beyond.

Accompaniment in the Final Stage of Life

An elderly widow becomes increasingly disoriented. Her children, who fear the onset of Alzheimer's disease or some other form of dementia, gradually find themselves unable to take care of her basic needs. Reluctantly, they decide to place her in a home for assisted living. A few months later, she has to be moved to the intensive-care wing of the home, and the children face the prospect of losing her. What kind of care can they and the medical personnel offer to accompany this woman most effectively and most compassionately through the final stage of life?

The needs such patients present are often spiritual as much as medical. If this woman is a believer, it is important for the family to establish close contact with her parish priest and with the facility's chaplain. In addition, they need to pay constant attention to their mother's spiritual and psychological states. As difficult as it is, it is important to address the matter of dying in a calm yet direct way. Does she feel fear or anxiety at the thought of reaching her life's end? If she were to die within the coming weeks or months, are there tasks still undone that she would like to accomplish, people she would want to speak with, or gatherings of friends and family she would like to plan? Are there people whose forgiveness she wants to seek and with whom she needs to be reconciled?

Then again, it is important to ask if her practical affairs are in order, if she has lists drawn up of possessions she would like to distribute or charitable acts she would want others to perform in her name. Has she made funeral plans, chosen the clothes she wants to be buried in, and revised her will? Does she want to be embalmed? Does she wish to donate any viable organs to other persons? And has the family contacted the funeral director to determine—before the crisis of death occurs, with all its tensions and grief—which coffin they will buy and how much the funeral home will be involved in the process of her burial? (Families are free to make their own choices and arrangements, although the funeral industry is reluctant to admit the fact.)[18]

More important than any of these questions, however, is the need for ongoing signs of compassion and love. As an elderly person

[18]Excellent resource material for helping a family deal with funeral and other arrangements following a death can be found in Lisa Carlson, *Caring for the Dead: Your Final Act of Love* (Hinesburg, VT: Upper Access, 1998). For the Funeral and Memorial Societies Association: www.funerals.org/famsa; 1–800–765–0107.

loses his grip on reality, forgets names and faces, and becomes increasingly immobile, his world shrinks in size, sometimes unbearably. Bedridden and ailing, he very often loses any sense of meaning to his existence and, consequently, any sense of hope. We cannot provide those values for him; preaching at this stage is simply not helpful. What is helpful is a loving and attentive presence: "You don't need to be afraid; I'm here." We can read psalms, if the person is inclined to listen, or we can simply sit and hold his hand.

If dementia is a problem, or simply failing mental capacity, it is important to engage the patient in various intellectual activities. Recent studies have confirmed that dementia in the elderly is significantly reduced by mental exercises: doing crossword puzzles, reading, playing musical instruments, singing, and the like. Significantly, no improvement was found in patients who simply increased their level of physical activity. The mind itself must be engaged. Sometimes the person can achieve this alone. More often it requires participation on the part of others. The patient may no longer be able to do the Sunday *Times* puzzle or play Scrabble, but even such simple activities as reading stories to grandchildren or strumming a guitar can lead to marked improvement in mental alertness and capacity.[19]

---

[19]See J. Verghese et al., "Leisure Activities and the Risk of Dementia in the Elderly," *New England Journal of Medicine* 348, no. 25 (June 19, 2003), cited in the *National Catholic Bioethics Quarterly* 3, no. 4 (Winter 2003): 800. This latter reference discusses the "Bronx Aging Study," which showed that mental activity among geriatric patients generates neurogenesis, strengthening existing synaptic connections in the brain.

As the person's infirmity progresses and she becomes increasingly unresponsive, we should remember that one of the last faculties to go is the ability to hear. One evening I entered a hospital room to visit an elderly woman who was comatose and clearly dying. Her brother announced my arrival to her, spoke a few gentle words into her ear, then stroked her forehead. She made no response whatsoever. Her eyes were closed and her breathing was shallow. She looked, in fact, as though she had already passed away. I put on a stole, took her hand in mine (it was cold as ice), then began reading from the Psalter. When I finished a few minutes later and closed the book, she squeezed my hand. There was no other sign of life, but it was clear that she was still there, still with us, as we were with her. As I was leaving, her brother came over, sat on the side of her bed, and waited until she died a couple of hours later.

That experience reminded me of other patients who have recovered from a coma and can repeat entire conversations held at the foot of their bed by family members or the doctors and nurses. Oblivious to the fact that comatose patients can often perceive sounds and comprehend speech, these people spoke of the patient's illness, or her prognosis, or her personality in ways they would never have done had she been obviously conscious. In order to avoid such gaffes but also to accompany someone appropriately, an important rule of thumb to remember is that unresponsive, comatose patients might well be listening.

In an article cited earlier, Father (now Bishop) Nikolaos Hatzinikolaou offers two complementary statements that need to be kept in mind by those who wish to accompany the terminally ill with faith and hope. "Artificial support is justifiable only when it offers therapy, prospect for life and hope for recovery to the patient"; and "Hope in the resurrection to eternal life is incomparably superior to the desperate struggle for the prolongation of earthly life."[20]

These are principles grieving family members need to keep in mind as they attempt to offer effective and appropriate care to a dying patient. Hospice workers recognize that the dying person is usually aware of their condition and that the most appropriate response is for the family to acknowledge the reality of the situation both to themselves and to the patient. Many people are reluctant to share the "bad news" of a diagnosis with someone who is terminally ill. In some cultures, including Russian, it is usually considered inappropriate or even cruel to share with the patient the fact that they have an incurable disease. This is a mistake. For Orthodox Christians especially, sufficient time is needed to prepare oneself in the face of impending death. This includes time to take stock of one's life and to offer what remains of it to God. As we noted earlier, it means seeking forgiveness and reconciliation, making confession, and receiving communion. For all of this, enough time is needed to stitch together, as it were, past and present as the person moves ineluctably toward God's future. To deprive a terminally ill patient of that time is to deprive him or her of a precious gift. That gift, however, can fulfill its purpose only when the announcement of some grave illness is accompanied by ongoing gestures of care and compassion. Tell the patient the truth, but tell it with love.

An important element in preparing for death is preparation of a living will or other advance directive. Like a DNR order, a living

[20]Hatzinikolaou, "Prolonging Life or Hindering Death?": 191, 195.

will can easily be overlooked or ignored, unless a proxy (a family member or friend with durable power of attorney) takes the initiative to bring the patient's wishes to the attention of the medical team. Another aunt of mine was confined to an elder-care wing of the local hospital for many years. As her condition deteriorated, she had "Do not resuscitate" marked on her medical chart. One day, trying to get out of bed, she fell, became unconscious, and suffered serious injury to her back and head. The doctor and nurses ignored the DNR order, and she spent the next ten years bedridden and semicomatose. If she had named a proxy, that person could have intervened. And her very real hope in the resurrection would have been fulfilled without her having to spend a decade in a near vegetative state.

Forms for living wills—which specify what sort of treatment we wish to have when and if we become terminally ill—are available in most hospitals and in many law offices. We should all fill one out, then their conditions should be made known, verbally or in writing, to those who might find themselves in a position to make life and death decisions on our behalf: parents or children, a trusted friend, a family doctor, and the parish priest.

A person who has entered the terminal stage of life can be most appropriately cared for by medical professionals who are trained in palliative care. This is most often and most effectively administered through some form of hospice program: in the hospital, in a residential facility, or at home. Hospice programs offer a much-needed alternative to the typical "American way of death," in which so often inappropriate and expensive therapies come into play (and often to prevent a lawsuit rather than to cure or relieve the patient). Because hospices accept only those patients who are in a terminal state, their medical teams have generally learned effective techniques for pain management, even with the most critical diseases such as cancer or ALS. They have learned that narcotics can be administered without creating addiction. (Though why should addiction even be a concern in terminal cases?) And they can usually prepare the family members for the grief that will inevitably follow the death of their loved one.

Returning to the question of nutrition and hydration in terminal cases, we find very often that patients diminish their intake of food and fluids toward the end and finally refuse them altogether. This should not be a cause for alarm. It can be a grave mistake and a serious injustice for the attending physician or nurse to rein-sert a feeding tube the patient has pulled out on the false assumption that the person is reacting to irritation or is suicidal. Before doing so, the doctor needs to determine clearly the motivation behind the patient's action. Some terminally ill patients in fact make the choice to die by refusing food and water, rather than to seek relief by some other means such as medically assisted suicide. In these cases, such a decision can be entirely appropriate. There comes a point when food no longer nourishes and merely hinders the body's progress toward a peaceful and relatively painless death. The decision at this stage of life to refuse food and to allow death to come more quickly than it otherwise would is not a choice for suicide. It is an appropriate response to the inevitable deterioration of bodily existence and should be respected as such, both by the medical team and by the Church.

A final word needs to be said about those who grieve the loss of a loved one, especially when those who bear that grief are children. Typically, as death approaches, the adults in a family become anxiously preoccupied with making arrangements for the funeral and dealing with their impending loss. Very often the children are ignored. A young child may be well aware that someone he loves is on the threshold of death and that the person will disappear forever from the child's life. In very young children, the reaction is often one of self-reproach, as if they themselves were responsible for the sickness or accident that is taking the loved one away. Once the death occurs, the grief these children feel can easily be compounded by guilt, and also by a sense of abandonment. "If she left me, I must have done something wrong." Guilt, abandonment, but also anger: "Why did she leave me? It's not fair!"

It is of the utmost importance, therefore, that children who are facing the loss of a person close to them be comforted and guided throughout the process leading up to and following the death. There are children's books that attempt to soften the blow and do so very effectively. Others, replete with pretty drawings of butterflies that die, then puppies, goldfish, and other pets, are much less successful. Attempting to send a soothing message, they in fact make a travesty of death and all that surrounds it. We must not forget that for a Christian, death is an enemy, a violent intrusion into God's good creation, whose consequences are a tearing apart of a person's being and the crushing weight of sadness borne by those who grieve. Death is an awesome and frightening mystery. Yet set in its proper perspective, it can be received as a wondrous occurrence, tragic yet filled with hope.

As an older person or a young sibling is dying, the family members can transform the situation for the child from one of bewilderment and tension into an opportunity for sharing the deepest convictions of their faith. They can speak to the child about the reality of death in terms the child can grasp. Avoiding frightening details of the dying process or of burial, they can convey to the child the love they themselves have for the person who has passed on, and confirm that person's continuing, unbroken love for the child. They can use the occasion, in other words, to lift the child, realistically but lovingly, out of despondency and give him hope. They can offer him the assurance that God's love is indeed stronger than death, that our ultimate hope is in the resurrection already accomplished by Christ, and that they, together with the departed loved one, are even now held in the embrace of our merciful and compassionate Father. This is nothing other than the message of the gospel, and the occasion of a death is an ideal time for introducing the child to the most poignant elements of that message, which speak of suffering, death, and life beyond.

The stages along life's way are many and varied. They differ with each person, from growth in the womb to the moment of death. They can be marked by tragedy as well as by joy: by abortion, violence, addiction, and illness, but also by creativity, delight in little things, acts of charity, and shared love. As life's journey comes to a close, especially when sickness and gradual physical deterioration provide the appropriate amount of time, we find ourselves called to prepare in a special way, with special intensity and focus, for the stage to come. That stage is what gives meaning to it all, providing direction and hope to our very being.

Without that hope, we can wallow in a "slough of despond," experiencing our daily existence as a living death. This is the condition so common among our contemporaries, good people who have never really heard the paschal promise of Christ's victory over sin, death, and corruption. For them, there is ultimately no meaning to life, a point driven home repeatedly by news reports of terrorism, war, genocide, corporate corruption, and natural disasters. If no distraction, no consuming passion, is adequate to fill the time, space, and prospects of their existence, they give in to depression and finally to despair. This attitude, this pathology so widespread in our day, led an acquaintance not long ago to compose a little poem that bears the title "One Dark Night."

> Maybe we should see the world as war
> And us as litter on a scorched and bloody field
> Strewn thickly with the nameless dead.
> Lonely corpses stripped of every shred
> Of purpose, hope or joy.
> Splintered bones and rotting flesh—
> Nothing more, nothing more.

This sad vision is shared by many people, and not only those who have rejected God as a matter of principle. It reflects the depression and loneliness that so easily wound those who have abandoned hope or never had it to begin with. The only meaningful reply to that tragically distorted perception of things has to be found in another way of viewing the world and our life within it. That is the way Christian tradition envisions life's movement, from stage to stage, from conception to the deathbed, as it leads toward fulfillment in the presence of God and in communion with the Holy Trinity.

The apostle Paul, obliged to fight his own demons, both within and without, gives us a glimpse of that final stage of our lives in a quotation that no biblical scholar has ever been able to identify. In his First Letter to the Corinthians (2.9), he speaks of a coming glory that "no eye has seen nor ear heard, nor the human heart has conceived." Yet this glory and this fulfillment, he declares, are precisely "what God has prepared for those who love him."

quotations used

Ch. 1: Bob Dylan, "The Times They Are A'Changin"; Archimandrite Sophrony, *Saint Silouan the Athonite* (Crestwood, NY: St Vladimir's Seminary Press, 1999), 434.

Ch. 2: Martin Buber, *I and Thou* (New York: Scribner's, 1958), 106.

Ch. 3: Donald DeMarco, Foreword to Jérôme Lejeune, *The Concentration Can* (San Francisco: Ignatius Press, 1992), ix.

Ch. 5: *The Wisdom of St Isaac the Syrian*, trans. by Sebastian Brock (Oxford: SGL Press, 1997), 19.

Ch. 7: Henri J. M. Nouwen, *Our Greatest Gift: A Meditation on Dying and Caring* (New York: HarperCollins, 1994), 103.